Dynamic
LIVING

Change Your Stinkin' Thinkin'

Principles4Freedom.com

Dynamic
LIVING

Change Your Stinkin' Thinkin'

JO ANN SCHROCK-HERSHBERGER

ISBN: 978-0-9904964-2-7

For additional copies contact:
JoAnn Hershberger
PO Box 162
Berlin, OH 44610

Layout & Design | Prisca Beachy

Carlisle Printing
OF WALNUT CREEK LTD
800.927.4196 · carlisleprinting.com
Sugarcreek, Ohio 44681

Dedicated to Merle,
THANK YOU!

Contents

Preface

For a long time I have been becoming more and more aware of my thought life. It is so easy to go through life and rarely think about the thoughts that run randomly through our minds. Our minds are moving constantly and often running from one thought to another so fast that we cannot track where the thoughts came from. One of the things I have done to train my mind and my thought life is to stop myself in the middle of a thought and then trace it back from the current thought to the thought before it to see where the thought came from. It is an amazing trip when you begin to do this. What it has taught me is that my mind can so quickly lead me down one path and instantly switch from that path to another one without me realizing what is happening. For an example I will catch a thought like remembering a conversation from yesterday and as I think about that conversation it leads me to thinking about the person I was talking to which then led me back to that persons brother and thinking about him which then led me back to think about where he works and what he does for a living which then led me to think about eating a taco at Taco Bell while I am at work. It's a crazy look at what is happening to our thought life and it does take practice. So catch your thought and allow your mind to take you back to what brought that thought and further back to what brought that thought and so on. I call it "thinking about what I am thinking about". Little by little I became more aware of my thoughts and learned that I can control my thoughts and I can stop my mind from going places it should not go. It isn't even so much that the exercise took me to thoughts I shouldn't have but it made me aware of how my thoughts lead me from one subject to another without me being aware of it.

All day every day our minds continue to roam from thought to thought. What would happen if we learned to keep our thoughts focused on God and what we have learned or are learning from His Word? How about keeping our mind fixed on Him and the wonderful life He has planned for us? What would happen if your mind was fixed on all God has done for you, how He saved you from your destructive ways, or how about thinking and focusing on the fact that God has promised us an abundant life? What would happen if instead of letting our minds roam freely we meditated on a scripture throughout the day, allowing it to sink into our being and becoming a part of who we are?

I have heard the idea of meditating on scripture compared to a cow chewing its cud. The cow will continue to chew and chew and chew on the same thing all day long. (A bit disgusting but…) That is what meditating is. People think they cannot meditate but if they are capable of worrying about something all day then they are already meditating, they are just meditating on the wrong thing.

If we take one scripture for a week and think about each word and take it in allowing it to speak to us we will start seeing truth in scripture that we do not easily see. Recently as I was reading through 2 Peter 1:1-10 I started to really look at each word. It is so easy to only hear the part that we are familiar with.

2 Peter 1:5-7 (NIV) *For this very reason, make every effort to add to your faith goodness; and to goodness, knowledge; and to knowledge, self-control; and to self-control, perseverance; and to perseverance, godliness; and to godliness, mutual affection; and to mutual affection, love.*

These verses from five to seven are things we have heard most of our Christian lives but what about what is in the verses just before and after these three verses. For instance in verse eight we find a truth we need to understand.

2 Peter 1:8 (NIV) *For if you possess these qualities in increasing measure, they will keep you from being ineffective and unproductive in your knowledge of our Lord Jesus Christ.*

If we want to live a life that is effective and productive in the knowledge of Christ then we need to care about these qualities being manifest in our lives.

What about the verses before verse 5?

2 Peter 1:3-4 (NIV) *His divine power has given us everything we need for a godly life through our knowledge of Him who called us by His own glory and goodness. Through these He has given us His very great and precious promises, so that through them you may participate in the divine nature, having escaped the corruption in the world caused by evil desires.*

According to these verses we have already been given these precious things if we have accepted Christ and His Holy Spirit. We have been given everything we need for a godly life through our knowledge of Him who called us. The promises are ours. We have already been given faith, goodness, knowledge, self control, perseverance and godliness. These are fruits of living this life; they are ours, we just need to claim them as ours. Often instead of knowing this we are trying in our own effort to live these things out in our lives. We fail to claim what is our inheritance!

So what would happen if we concentrated on these things and meditated on them day and night? We are told to bind the words of God around our necks and write them on the tablets of our hearts, how does that look and are we even close to doing that?

Instead of meditating on these things we meditate by worrying about things we have no control over. We need to quit wasting our time with those thoughts. They do us no good and solve nothing but they do prove that yes you can indeed meditate because I am sure there is not one person who is reading this that isn't guilty of meditating in this way. Stop thinking on these negative things and renew your thinking to line up with God's Word. Meditate, chew on the words over and over till they produce life in you and they become a part of your inmost being.

If you put forth the effort to change your thinking and take charge of your thoughts you will find that you worry less, you are less stressed and you will sleep better because worry will not keep you awake at night.

My dad use to say that if you could just take a new Christian and plug a hose into one ear and wash out all the old ways of thinking and start fresh with a new way of thinking (he called it stinkin' thinkin') then our lives would be easier. Unfortunately that doesn't work so well but we can have a new life with a new way of thinking. Clean out the old thoughts and replace those thoughts with the truth of God's Word and you will have a new life.

So I encourage you to take this journey with me and take charge of your thoughts, change your life by taking the next step with a new way of thinking and get rid of your stinkin' thinkin'. There is a better life waiting for you!

When it came to a title for this book I struggled for a few weeks. The book didn't go to print because I just didn't know what to call it. I had a list of names but none of them stood out to me. Then one day I remembered my dads involvement in an organization he and John Ruth started many years ago.

It was called Dynamic Living. I mentioned it to my mother and let it lay for a few weeks then I met up with John Ruth and he started talking about Dynamic Living. I asked him where the name came from and he told me about how he and dad were talking about the fact that the church is not teaching us how to live with every day circumstances such as hard work, dependability and honesty. John and dad decided to start this organization and they did recordings on cassette tapes to teach these things. John said that when he told dad about this dad got excited because he understood that people needed to be taught these things, he got so excited he did two somersaults! I guess he was really excited. So I have named this book *Dynamic Living* in memory of my father and his hard work in trying to teach all of us to change our stinkin' thinkin'. My fathers life message was that Christians are called to be salt and light in a dark world.

Acknowledgments

I want to honor God in all that I do. "Thank you Father for allowing me to do something I so enjoy doing. I would never have thought I would put words on paper for others to read and maybe I learn more from writing those words than others who read them but it has been a wonderful experience and I am thankful for it. As long as you put words in my heart to share I will share them but help me to always know when the words are my words instead of your words, written on my own efforts. If my writing helps one person find you it will all have been worth it. It is not your will that any should perish and I want to make a difference to someone. Thank you Father for loving me and being with me on these wonderful journeys and for the inspiration you are to me. I want to be a vessel that is used and makes a difference."

Thank you to my Redeemer, my Savior. Thank you also to those who God has put in my path who have been such a great asset to me. I want to say a special thank you to my dear friend Janice Strawn who is not afraid to correct me when I am wrong in my thinking. "We all need someone like you in our lives, I am glad God has given you to me". I am truly blessed. To Dr. David Migliore who has always encouraged me to overcome and go further, thank you for writing the introduction for this book. I really appreciate your time and your kind words. Thank you also to Bernie Torrence, your support throughout the years has been wonderful and you are greatly appreciated. Your encouragement makes the journey enjoyable.

I am not an author. I make no claims and take no credit for any of the books I have written. When I first felt that God was calling me to write I sat down at the computer with a book in mind. I knew I was called to write a book about my father so I decided to take the plunge and start. The words did not come. I knew I was not an author.

Not until after my father passed away did the words come. When God was in it and the time was right, writing became an absolute joy. I enjoyed every minute of the journey. I loved remembering the days of growing up in the household of John and Marie Schrock. I loved being reminded of days gone by, of time spent in church, of relationships that were developed and friendships being made that lasted a lifetime. I fell in love with writing.

Although I enjoyed the journey I had no intentions of ever writing a second book. I had no inspiration or desire to write anything. I knew I was not an author. Then God dropped a thought into my mind and my mind wouldn't stop until I sat down at the computer and began a second book. Again when the time was right God was in it. The words flowed almost effortlessly. It was again a joy to write a book. However I was still not an author.

"Change Begins with Me" was the result of my second attempt at writing. Just as with the first book I loved it, but I knew it was not in me to write a book. People called me an author and I finally accepted that maybe I was an author but I really think I am just a co-author! I knew that on my own I was not a writer. All I had to do was remember my first attempt at writing and know it was not a natural gift.

So here goes my third book! I again had no idea I would write a third book, no plans at all. God again dropped an idea into my spirit and the words came. I asked myself why God would want me to write books. I am uneducated, not a person with big words or much knowledge yet God chose me to write three books. I can only give God credit because I know what I am capable of and I know I am not an author without Him. Recently I was reminded of a prophetic word that was given to me and it brought a smile to my face to realize that what was said has indeed come to pass. I was told that I would write books. How wonderful to have a Father who knows my future and it is good, He knows me so much better than I know myself!

I have found that with God all things truly are possible. I have finally come to a point that if God says I am an author, so be it. However I have no desire to write without Him. As I write this current book I am constantly asking God what I have missed, what have I overlooked, is there anything else I should be adding to this book? I let it rest a few days and a thought enters my mind and I again sit at the computer and begin to write. I have at times thought to myself "I really should take some time to write today" and as surely as I do when I sit down there are no words. So I close up the computer and wait to hear from God. This book has taken longer than I originally thought because of the times I have thought it was done but then I would hear more and continue to add to it. It is now getting ready to go to print and I cannot help but wonder if there is still more. Maybe I'll wait a few more weeks just in case...

La Red has also become a big part of my life and I have studied the principles and tried to apply them to my life the best I can and I am always learning more and seeing more areas where I need to refine and do better. The principles of La Red as written by my father bring about a new way of thinking. That is the purpose of them. For life to work as God meant it to work we need to change how we think and how we see things. The forty principles when studied over a period of a year in a round table setting or in the on-line course change how you think. You begin to see that there is a better way of doing things. You start thinking of the other person, you start thinking about what is right rather than who is right. It is the beginning of a new life, one of victory. For more information on La Red visit them on the web at www.lared.org. You can also find information there on the on line course called Global Entrepreneurs Institute.

It is time to change our stinkin' thinkin' and live the way God created us to live!

Introduction

Dynamic Living
"Change your Stinkin' Thinkin'"

Jo Ann's 3rd book, that which you are about to read, is more than a book. It is a "handbook" of overcoming the challenges, struggles and circumstances we face in a culture and society that is on a downward spiral.

And overcoming begins with our "Stinkin' Thinkin'".

All through (this book/Dynamic Living) Jo Ann gives directions, insights and scriptures that will assist you in the challenges that we all face. We are living in a world that is over stimulated with technology. Massive information is exchanged on an hourly basis in the young minds of our children. From an early age our minds are corrupted by the input of a world that is further and further away from God.

We are transformed by the renewing of our minds. This is necessary because our minds through our input from the world are corrupted. Each minute we have access to a world that is rotting away. Unless we learn to become aware of our thoughts, which are a product of our input, we will fail to be transformed from the inside out.

Input produces thoughts, thoughts produce feelings, feelings produce actions, actions create habits, and habits produce our destiny.

…Then it only makes sense that our thought lives have gone amuck, and the product of our thinking is a destiny not intended for those called by God.

The input we receive from cell phones, face book, television, social media is changing our lives for the worse. If we are to live in an abundant life, which Jesus came here for us to have, we must understand that it will all start with our thought lives. If we are to overcome "the issues of life", which are products of our thinking, then we have got to know the way *"that few there be find"*.

Move forward into the solution that Jo Ann presents into a deeper understanding of the significance of our thought life. Learn through her teachings and scriptures how to overcome the world that has been created in our minds from all the negative ungodly input. Absorb the many relevant scriptures Jo Ann provides as she walked through the difficulties of her life. Assimilate the teachings, scriptures and lessons into your mind so you can have what Jesus came here for.

Live an Abundant life. Renew your mind. Change your stinking thinking. Overcome.

"To him that overcomes, he will sit next to me on my throne"

You have "the way" presented in Jo Ann's book, to sit next to the King of the Universe.

How will you answer this call?

Dr. David Migliore D.D.S., PhD
Dean of Students Global Entrepreneurs Institute
President Practice Principles International

1

The Good Shepherd

· MY SHEEP KNOW MY VOICE ·

Who am I? We are accustomed to people asking us who we are. We tell them who our parents are, who are spouse is or what we do for a living. But none of those tells anyone who you are. We think of ourselves only as earthly beings and we have a hard time seeing ourselves as God sees us. When God looks at us He doesn't see someone's spouse, someone's son or daughter nor does He see you as someone with any specific employment. What does God see when He looks at a believer and what makes a person a child of God?

As believers God sees Jesus when He looks at us. We are sons and daughters of God and Jesus is our brother. God loves us and desires very much to have a relationship with us. A relationship cannot happen without communication. A married couple has to have communication to have a relationship. Friends have to have communication to have a friendship. The same is true of you and God; you cannot have a relationship or friendship without communication. God talks to everyone but not everyone hears Him, they do not have their ears tuned to hear Him, they are not receptive.

Salvation comes when we choose to accept what God has done for us. He sent His son to come to earth and show us the way. It is up to us to believe in the mission of the Son and to believe that He is the true son of God, that He lived on earth as a man born of a virgin. We choose to believe that He was crucified, buried and resurrected. We choose to believe that He is seated at the right hand of the Father because His work is completed. He did what was asked of the Father and now we worship and adore Him for what He has done for us. We believe all of this in our hearts and we confess it with our mouth. We are not ashamed of the Good News that He delivered to us. The day will come when He returns to the earth again to gather all those who have chosen to believe and take them to a home He has prepared for those who believe, in heaven.

We are all born into a fallen world with a fallen nature. God's son Jesus came to earth to redeem anyone who would choose to follow Him, as a human we all have the right and the ability to make that choice. Some of us will choose to follow, others won't. Jesus came to earth leaving a home far beyond our imagination. He is the very Son of God who lived in heaven with the Father before coming to earth. I imagine Jesus in heaven where He was praised and loved by a Father who absolutely adored His Son. God also loved and adored the human beings He had created on earth and decided to send His Son to redeem us so that we could have fellowship with the Father who created us. Meanwhile on earth there was Satan who had control of the earth after he had been thrown out of heaven and he was and is determined to keep as many as he can from accepting the redemption that is being offered. He works overtime to keep us roaming around without knowing we have a Father who loves us and wants us to have an abundant life. Satan on the other hand is out to destroy our lives.

John 10:10 (NIV) *¹⁰The thief comes only to steal and kill and destroy; I have come that they may have life, and have it to the full.*

The Father wants to have communication with the humans He created. When He created man He told him to take dominion over the earth and all that was in it. God wants to talk to us and He wants us to talk to Him. He is there at all times to help us make decisions and right choices. Satan on the other hand doesn't want us to know what God is offering to us and he doesn't want us to know that we can have a very real relationship with God through Jesus.

In the Old Testament God gave us a long list of laws to abide by, laws that were impossible to keep. The law was given to help us see that we on our own can never live as holy as we should. We all have missed the target holiness. The New Testament was the new way, a better way through the Son of God.

Ephesians 3:23-25 *²³Before the coming of this faith, we were held in custody under the law, locked up until the faith that was to come would be revealed. ²⁴So the law was our guardian until Christ came that we might be justified by faith. ²⁵Now that this faith has come, we are no longer under a guardian.*

Galatians 2:20-21 *²⁰I have been crucified with Christ and I no longer live, but Christ lives in me. The life I now live in the body, I live by faith in the Son of God, who loved me and gave Himself for me. ²¹I do not set aside the grace of God, for if righteousness could be gained through the law, Christ died for nothing!"*

Christ came to earth for us, for our salvation and He wants a relationship with us. Think about what it would be like if you went to some faraway place to help people in need, you left your home where you had every convenience and family who loved you. In this far away place people would not want to talk to you, to give you a chance to help them. You would give anything to help them have a better life and you knew what needed to be done to help them but they refused to communicate with you. We are in no way Jesus but this might help us to understand that for us to receive what Jesus has made available we need communication. He wants to talk to us and tell us things.

John 10:27 (NIV) *27My sheep listen to my voice; I know them, and they follow me.*

Sheep are interesting animals. Throughout the Bible believers are referred to as sheep and the Lord is referred to as the shepherd. Sheep follow a shepherd and trust that the shepherd will lead them to safety, water and shade as needed. They do not question where they are being led but happily follow the shepherd. It is a sheep's natural tendency to follow; they will follow another sheep even when it leads to their death. As believers we should be following Jesus as easily as a sheep follows its leader with complete trust. We should trust that God knows what He is doing, He wants only the best for us and we can safely follow Him wherever He leads us.

Many times God will only lead us to the next step but until we take that step we will not know what is next. God wants our complete trust. We have an enemy that wants to destroy us likewise sheep have many natural enemies like coyotes, mountain lions, wolves and domestic dogs. Sheep are a timid and defenseless animal and they totally rely on the shepherd for their safety. We are to be like sheep and we are to follow the Good Shepherd totally relying on Him to meet our needs.

A shepherd's calm reassuring voice calms the sheep when they became restless or afraid. Jesus does the same for us. A good shepherd cares greatly for his sheep and at the end of a day of roaming and grazing he will count all of his sheep making sure he hasn't lost any. If any are missing he will go in search of them. Each morning the shepherd will lead his sheep out for grazing in a good pasture and as the day gets hot he will lead them to cool areas where they will have access to water. A good shepherd is dependable, diligent and brave. He will even risk his life for his sheep. Our God is the same and gave His life for us. All we now have to do is to follow His voice, a voice we need to become familiar with. We need to build that relationship and that takes communication. Spend time with God reading His Word; praise Him with songs of praise or your own words. Talk to Him like you would a friend because that is what He wants to be, your friend.

If we know the voice of the Father and have a relationship with Him we will know when the voice we are hearing is not Him just like sheep know the voice of their shepherd. Two or three flocks of sheep can be herded together and will easily separate themselves from each other when they hear the voice of their shepherd. I love this picture! We should be just like this. We should have complete trust in our Father, our Shepherd and easily follow His voice when we hear it. If you are in doubt as to whether you are hearing from God or not, there are several things you can do to verify that you are hearing from Him. God's direction to you will never go against His Word, does what you hear line up with the Bible? Does the answer bring you peace, complete peace? If not, do not depend on the word you received being from God. God's word brings peace not turmoil.

Now that we know a bit about hearing from God we also need to understand how God loves us and all He did for us. I am sure none of us completely understands this and I doubt that we will ever get it clearly before we get to heaven but it is my desire to understand this as clearly as I am able to in this life. I think if we really understood the love of the Father for us our lives would be completely different, we would think differently and act differently. I believe that God wants to walk and talk to us, to have clear lines of communication with us so that we can understand His love but we have trouble comprehending it all.

If we have accepted Jesus as Lord of our lives then God does not see the filthiness of our human existence. When He looks at us He sees what Jesus has done for us and He sees us as His dearly loved children. This realization alone should bring about a new way of thinking. If we are believers then we should see ourselves the way God sees us, not condemned but redeemed! We are redeemed and are in right standing with God because of Jesus. We do not need to be afraid of God. God's wrath will not be against His followers. God is love, the very essence of love. When we get our minds renewed to this truth the rest of the journey to renewing our minds becomes easier. We will think differently because we see ourselves differently.

I love the song that states, "I am forgiven at the foot of the cross, I've been accepted by the blood of the lamb, my every stain is washed away I've been for forgiven." To be forgiven, what a load that takes off of us. We do not have to carry guilt with us. Jesus has taken it all upon Himself and we walk in newness of life because of His sacrifice.

Let's start the process of renewing our minds by renewing how we see God and taking in all the love He has for us. Let us see that we are valued by God and He only wants what is best for us. He will never lead us to the wrong place and never leave our side. He is with us at all times and He hears every prayer you pray whether you feel that your prayer reached Him or not. He is talking to us but we can miss His voice by not knowing it is Him speaking.

If we can get these things clear in our heads and let them sink into our hearts our minds will follow and be renewed, but first we have to believe.

2

Knowing Who You Are

· WE ARE CREATED IN GOD'S OWN IMAGE ·

Believing that you are a child of God is the key to understanding who you are. We know it in our heads but not always in our hearts. Once the realization of this truth penetrates our very being our thinking makes big changes. Believe that you are truly a child of God, that He really is your Father. This is a Father that loves like no other. He wants only what is good for you, He wants you to prosper, He wants you to succeed, He wants you to feel loved. He adores you! He has your name written on His hand. Don't worry about how He can possibly have all believers' names written on His hand; just believe it because His word says it is so.

Isaiah 49:15-16 (NIV)

15 "Can a mother forget the baby at her breast
   and have no compassion on the child she has borne?
Though she may forget,
   I will not forget you!
16 See, I have engraved you on the palms of my hands;
   your walls are ever before me.

I think too many times we try to make sense of things that

are beyond our understanding. We have to trust that God is smarter than we are and if He says our names are written on His hands then it's true. We don't need to second guess Him or understand everything. We need to be like a child that just believes because daddy said so.

There is someone I admire in the Old Testament. This was before Jesus came to redeem us but this man understood who his Father was and he simply believed! This man is Daniel. His is an amazing story. We read the Bible and don't always try to imagine what it would have been like to be there. We need to let our imaginations go a bit and picture what his life might have been like.

He was a teenager when he was taken (kidnapped) from his home. He was separated from his family and taken to a completely foreign country. Nothing in his new home was in any way like the home he was taken from. He was an Israelite. He knew the stories of the great men of God like Abraham and Moses. He knew the history of his people. He was surrounded by friends and family. He was taught about a God who was greater than anyone he had ever met, but he had never seen Him in person. The stories he was taught about his ancestors told him how big God was.

His home was secure, he was loved by his family, he worshiped in the synagogue, he grew up with his cousins, and Daniel had a good life.

Taken from his home and waking up in a foreign country against his will would not have been an easy adjustment. He had no doubt heard of these people and heard stories about how evil they were. He heard that they worshipped idols, they trusted in magicians, astrologers, and enchanters. They didn't hesitate to put people to death for not obeying the king.

They placed him with the eunuchs and may possibly have made him a eunuch, and they made plans for his life. Daniel had no say as to what would happen to him but he believed in a God that was able to deliver. He could have gone with the crowd. Thousands were taken but we hear only of a few of them in the Bible. I'm sure many followed the ways of their new surroundings. I would imagine that most would have fought against it at first but with time they yielded to the ways of their new home. Not Daniel, he never wavered. It's not easy to keep standing when everyone around you is "doing it". We tend to give in to easily and become like the world around us. In Daniels case only a few remained strong. The pressure of going with the crowd, possibly with other family members and friends would have been great. We can all learn a lesson from Daniel. He knew who he was, he stood up for what he believed, and his life made a difference. Here we are thousands of years later still learning from his example.

When Daniel was told he would be served food that he knew he shouldn't eat he found favor and was permitted to eat the diet he wanted. Many would have thought "it's just food, lets enjoy". Because he stood for what he believed God blessed him and at the end of ten days he was healthier than all the others who had eaten the king's food.

Before the exile we have no record of Daniel ever interpreting dreams. However when the king was going to kill all the wise men of the kingdom because they couldn't tell him his dream and interpret it, God used Daniel to spare the lives of all the wise men. Daniel was calm and he understood who he was. He understood who his Father was and he knew his Father was able to deliver no matter what the circumstances. Daniel was a blessing to the kingdom and in the end even Nebuchadnezzar king of Babylon became a believer in the one true God! Take time to read all of Daniels story in the Old Testament book of Daniel.

We do not know what our stand for truth and godliness will do to change the world. Daniel just did what was right; it wasn't a hard decision for him because he knew who he was. Often our choices become hard because we do not understand who we are.

Daniel's mind was fixed on his Creator. He lived in exile but he did not change. He was exposed to every sin known to mankind but he remained strong because of what he knew. All of this and he was just a teenager!

We need to believe and know like Daniel knew. This was all before Jesus, we have more than Daniel did yet our minds are not where his was. We need to renew our minds and know who we are just as Daniel did.

Every aspect of our lives needs to change. How we talk, think, how we spend our money, how we love, how we see others, and so much more will all change as we become new on the inside.

Let's start with believing what the Word of God says about who we are, let's fix our minds on our Father and trust Him to be who He says He is, the rest will follow.

When I consider who I am I think of the song "Good Good Father" by Chris Tomlin. The words tell me that He is a good, good Father and then go on to say "I am loved by Him, it's who I am" This truth of who I am is becoming more real to me all the time. To understand that I am truly and purely loved by God is almost overwhelming. I remember a time many years ago when I was going through a very difficult time in my life and I was crying out to God just to be able to bear the load. I was driving at night and I clearly saw the eyes of Jesus before me looking at me with more love than is explainable. It was as though He knew me better than I knew myself and He still loved me. He knew all about me, my mistakes, my bad habits, my sin, and He still loved me. He fully understood everything I was going through.

I will never forget that night but no matter how hard I try I have not been able to see those eyes again, but I remember the depth of the love and what it did for my broken spirit. I am loved by God! That is who I am and everything else I may be falls to the wayside as I dwell on this truth and this truth alone.

John 15:9 (NIV) *9 "As the Father has loved me, so have I loved you."*

Did you get that? Read it again and let it sink in. How much do you think God loves His Son? Are there any words to describe the depth of His love for his Son? That is how Jesus loves us. Our lives would drastically change if we could grasp just how much we are loved.

I am part of God's plan for such a time as this. There is a very real purpose for my time on earth, I am not a mistake or an afterthought, I was created on purpose for these times, and so were you.

Psalm 139:13-16 (NIV)

13 For you created my inmost being;
*   you knit me together in my mother's womb.*
14 I praise you because I am fearfully and wonderfully made;
*   your works are wonderful,*
*   I know that full well.*
15 My frame was not hidden from you
*   when I was made in the secret place,*

when I was woven together in the depths of the earth.
¹⁶Your eyes saw my unformed body;
    all the days ordained for me were written in your book
    before one of them came to be.

When I do what God has asked me to do I am taking steps towards the future God has planned for me. I am sure I have taken many side trips because I haven't always understood the things I now understand and I hate to say it but I may take a few more side trips before I actually accomplish my main purpose on earth.

When I read a scripture like Psalm 139 I am overwhelmed that God had a specific plan for my life before I was born. Actually in Ephesians one it says that he chose us before the world was made, he had plans for us before time began! I think about what that path might have looked like and I wonder how far off track I have been at times. God's plan for my life is incredible and more wonderful than I can imagine. How far off track am I, how often have I crossed the path, what have I missed because of my own selfish plans?

With each side trip I take I learn things, I learn more about myself and more about my creator. I gain more understanding about other people and the hurts and pains of life. I become more understanding of the problems of others because of the things I have faced throughout my own life. I am being refined by a refiner's fire and I must say it is often painful. Just as gold is refined by high heat so am I being refined by the fire, to become pure and Christ like.

Life might be painful and refining may be hard but through it all I am loved by the Master of the universe who has incredible plans for my life and yours!

3

How We Think Makes a Difference

· AS A MAN THINKS IN HIS HEART ·

Eternity, how does it look? It is beyond what we as humans can comprehend yet as believers we know it is real and we will live for eternity. The only visual I can think of is a circle that has no beginning or end, it continues forever. If we look at the circle as eternity, the way God created it, then take a slice out of it called "time" we can get a glimpse of Gods plan for mankind. At the end of time we will once again go into eternity, life without end.

God created time with seconds, minutes, hours, days, weeks and years. All of this will end when Christ returns. This period is called "the end of the Age". Each person when they were born into this world entered a spirit life that will go into eternity. Not everyone believes this but it doesn't make it any less real. Many people don't believe that God exists but in the same way it doesn't make Him any less real. All one has to do is to look at the world around us and see creation to know that there is a God.

Romans 1:20 (NIV) *²⁰For since the creation of the world God's invisible qualities—His eternal power and divine nature—have been clearly seen, being understood from what Has been made, so that people are without excuse.*

Seriously look around you, do you really think that all of this happened by some explosion and then it all just came together so perfectly that it all works in perfect harmony? How could anyone believe that? It is obvious that there is a greater being, God!

I believe that when a baby is born, that first breath they take is God breathing into them. God is the creator of life which begins at conception, but it is only after the baby is out of the womb that the breath of God enters him. He has given us this wonderful gift called life, and we are to use it to bring glory to His name. We are made up of three parts, body, soul and spirit. We can see our body and the soul we have is our emotions and feelings but our spirit is the part that connects to God. For each of us "time" begins with the first breath we take and it ends with the last breath we take. At that point we enter into eternity. Only then will we fully understand what eternity looks like.

My father lives in eternity, as do many of your loved ones that have passed on before us. They understand things that we do not; they see things that we cannot even imagine. We are told in scripture the earth is a shadow of heaven so I see heaven as being a beautiful version of the earth with vivid color and wonderful activities to satisfy all of our likes. God made each of us with different likes and dislikes and I believe that if you loved gardening on earth you will love it even more in heaven, if you enjoyed hiking, camping, painting or whatever I believe those will be the same things you will enjoy in heaven. You will hike more beautiful mountains, camp beside more peaceful rivers and see more beautiful waterfalls, the sky may become a canvas for the artist, who knows, and I just know it will be beyond anything we can begin to imagine.

With the time that we have been given here on earth, God has given us the right to choose how we will live, how we will spend the time He has given us. The time is short and will be gone before we know it. As a teenager I thought it took forever till my next birthday, today I realize that the years have flown by and they seem to go faster each year. I am sure many reading this understand what I am talking about. If you are like me you have had birthdays you don't even remember!

In the natural it seems that time will always be. We cannot imagine a world without time. We live by the clock. It tells us when to get up, when we have to be somewhere, and when to go to bed. It tells us when we have a birthday, when spring break comes, and when winter begins. Time tells us when it is time to retire from a job, when we should downsize and simplify life. Our whole world revolves around time. In our humanness we cannot relate to anything different. Our inability to relate doesn't change the fact that time will end and that there is an eternity that we will all face at some time.

In the meantime, we live our time on earth with choices. We face choices every day. It seems that the world we live in has more choices with each passing year. I am amazed at the things my grandchildren are facing as teenagers today. I had more than enough choices of things to do that would get me in trouble as a teen and today there is so much that is readily available to them it's almost scary. They are facing things that never entered my mind. Who would have thought that the internet would become so readily available that our children would all carry around mini computers and have access to the entire world! We need to pray for our teens and as parents we need to be involved in their lives, they need godly guidance daily. Peer pressure can so easily put them at risk for things that can destroy their lives in a very short time. The choices they face and the opportunities that lie before them are overwhelming. Teenagers are inexperienced but they often feel invincible and unless we get involved early in their lives guiding with clear and godly thinking they can be headed for serious trouble early in life. Their thinking needs to be right from a young age. Get involved and help steer them in the right direction.

Even as adults we can make some poor choices and ruin our lives. We see shattered lives all around us, choices made by adults that destroyed not only them but their families. At the same time we see the results of the good choices others have made. How do we keep ourselves on the right path and know that our choices are really going to lead us where we want to go?

What is the key, how do we make sure we are doing the right thing? There appears to be a lot of hidden agendas in the world today and even in elections we do not truly know what we are voting for. The piles of papers that are included in some of these new proposals and laws are so extensive that no one really looks at all the details that are included in any new law. We vote things into laws without knowing all the details. In life we face challenges every day, and choices have to be made, often without thinking very long we jump to a conclusion, making a choice without all the information we need to make a wise decision. We don't always take time to think about the details. Even then our decisions are based on the information in our heads. The things we have heard or read all play a part in how we make decisions.

Important decisions should be brought to our Father. We need to talk to Him about the decisions we face. Tell Him about the problem then pray and read the Word listening for an answer. Do not make important decisions quickly but take time and wait on God for instruction.

Without values, principles and knowledge of God's will for our lives, there is no way to make sound judgments or good choices. If we do not have a good understanding of God's ways of doing things it is easy to make a bad decision.

When we get saved and accept Jesus as our Lord we are told to change the way we think. Unfortunately most new Christians accept the Savior but then are not taught anything beyond salvation. That may be the church's fault or it may be the new believers fault. Either way there is much more to Christianity. We still have to live on earth and be a part of this life. The challenge for us comes in living in this world but not loving the ways of the world. In other words we should not be caught up in the things of the world.

John 17:15-16 (NIV) *¹⁵My prayer is not that you take them out of the world but that you protect them from the evil one. ¹⁶They are not of the world, even as I am not of it.*

New Christians have been ensured a home in heaven but what about this life? Jesus told us He came to give us life and to give it more abundantly. He was talking about this life not our eternal life. Here and now we are to have an abundant life. Life was meant to be good. We are to have peace and joy, yet we see so little of the effects of this kind of life. What is wrong that we live without these benefits that we are told in the Word of God would be ours? Where are we going wrong? And how is it even possible to live in peace when so many things are going wrong in our world?

Families are falling apart, we live with divorce all around us and it seems rare to see marriages that last for twenty years. There is no peace in this kind of a life. How is it possible to have peace with all of this happening? Did Jesus really mean it when he said "I have come that you might have life and have life more abundantly"? So many Christians have no idea how to obtain this kind of a life, they have heard it said, but they do not have a clue how to get to that life. What needs to change to be able to fulfill and live this abundant life?

It starts with our thinking!

Romans 12:2 (NIV) *²Do not conform to the pattern of this world, but be transformed by the renewing of your mind. Then you will be able to test and approve what God's will is—His good, pleasing and perfect will.*

Our minds need to be transformed. We have spent our entire lives thinking about ourselves, making us happy, pleasing ourselves. We are selfish, rude and very seldom think of anyone else's happiness. Today we live in a world that believes everyone can live however they feel is right in their own eyes. Yes we certainly need to transform our selfish self centered minds. We need to know what is pleasing and perfect in the eyes of God. Without the mind of Christ how can we possibly know how to make good choices or what is good and pleasing to God? God has provided us with an owner's manual that tells us the answers to these questions. Any time you buy a new appliance it comes with an owner's manual and if you want to know all that the equipment you bought can do you will take time to read the manual. How will you ever get all you paid for if you don't know the information in the manual? Very few of us would consider using our new equipment without spending time reading the manual. Those of us who decide to do without the manual usually end up in trouble and then we have to go back and read it to find out what we are doing wrong.

As Christians we often do the same thing. We depend on the preacher at church to tell us what we need to know not understanding that the Owners Manuel has a lot more in it than the preacher will get to in a year. Too many times it is not until our lives fall apart that we dig out the Manual and try to fix whatever has gone wrong. Only then do we take it seriously. How much better would it be if we started with the Owner's Manual and applied the directions before a disaster hits our lives? Our Bibles have the answers we need.

When we receive Christ as our Lord and Savior we are given a new life. However if we don't read the Owner's Manual that comes with the instructions and the wisdom that we need to get all of this life that has been promised then we shouldn't expect to have the abundant life that comes with our salvation. Read the Manual and you will see that there is so much more life for us than we are actually living. Don't wait till life isn't working to get the Manual out and start reading it.

Some people will say that the Bible is too hard to understand. With all the translations now available you can find one that suits you. There is no good excuse to not own a Bible that you can understand. A good pastor will help you to understand what you do not understand, get involved in a good Bible teaching church and attend with the attitude that you are going to learn something rather than attending because it makes you look good. Looking good does not do anything to improve your life!

Most of us have been taught that we must not be like the world but many have never been told that you do this with a new way of thinking. There are groups of people who look around them and they see that the world lives with modern conveniences and things like TVs and computers and they decide that these are the ways of the world so they eliminate these things from their lives in order to not be like the world. You can remove anything from your life in the natural, move to an area "off the grid" but no matter where you go your mind goes with you. There is nothing wrong with modern conveniences. There is good that can come from them but if our thinking isn't right these same things can have a very negative effect on our lives. I can still hear my father say "Things in themselves are not wrong but what we do with the things is what is wrong." A computer is neither good nor bad, it is just a computer. However you can take that computer and look at pornography or you can use Bible Gateway and learn about God. There is a big difference in what a corrupt mind will do with a computer and what a mind that has been renewed will do with the same computer. If we don't change our habits and our thinking we will continue down the wrong path even though we have met the Savior.

We have many years of wrong thinking that we need to change. The old way of thinking is what messed up our life to begin with and if we do not change the way we think we will still have all the same problems we had before we were saved. Without this change you will never live the abundant life Jesus was talking about.

Matthew 7:13-14 (NIV) *13"Enter through the narrow gate. For wide is the gate and broad is the road that leads to destruction, and many enter through it. 14But small is the gate and narrow the road that leads to life and only a few find it.*

Here we read that there is a wide gate and road as well as a narrow gate and a narrow road. Notice that there are few that find the narrow way that leads to life.

John 10:10 (NIV) *¹⁰The thief comes only to steal and kill and destroy; I have come that they may have life, and have it to the full.*

Now we see that not only are we looking for the narrow way that leads to life but we are told about a full life that can and should be ours, a way Jesus came to make available for us.

Romans 12:2 (NIV) *²Do not conform to the pattern of this world, but be transformed by the renewing of your mind. Then you will be able to test and approve what God's will is—his good, pleasing and perfect will.*

Here we see that we have to change how we think. Can all of this be related to the full life that we are told about? God has a good, pleasing and perfect will for our lives but we will not find that life without changing how we think. God never asks us to do what cannot be done and we are told repeatedly throughout the Word of God that all things are possible with God. Our problem is we try to accomplish things without His help.

We read a scripture like Matthew 7 and look at the impossibility of living and walking the narrow road. We feel overwhelmed at the thought that "few there be that find it" but again with God it can be done and it can be how we live our lives. If we follow the scriptures listed above we can see how one can lead to the next and we can find life and find it to the full. We can travel on the narrow road that leads to life.

Let's go to the beginning and follow this through. First we get saved, we learn to change our thinking and it transforms us. This new way of thinking helps us to line up with the Word of God and we find the narrow way, the one that cannot be found outside of God. The narrow way now leads us to the abundant life that is promised to us. The things that previously filled our lives are no longer of interest as we learn to see that they are damaging to our lives. As we eliminate these habits from our lives the way becomes clearer. Our choices become less because our desires change. This is not a hard thing to live with instead it simplifies everything about life. By changing our thinking and renewing our mind we find the narrow way and on the narrow way we find the abundant life. One does not happen without the other. They are all linked together but it starts with a new way of thinking.

If our lives do not feel full and abundant then we need to go back and check out our thinking. Is our thinking out of line with the Word of God? If you are not spending time in the Word you cannot possibly know what the Word of God is. Going to church on Sunday and listening to a twenty to thirty minute sermon is not going to change your thinking. Your thinking has to be dealt with all week, every day and at times every minute of every day.

The more time you spend in the Word the more understanding you will get. You will also find that the more time you spend in the Word the more time you will want to spend in the Word. The Word is seed and it grows and as it grows in you it changes you from the inside out. As understanding begins to dawn you find that you want even more understanding. Little by little you can see change coming to your life, you react differently, you aren't as critical, you are kinder to others, you start caring about others, and you develop compassion for them. Your thinking changes and you start to see the good in life as you renew your mind. The seed that you are planting in your spirit grows in the new environment of your spirit because the Word you are taking in is alive.

As God becomes more central in your life you start to see Him as a loving Father. You start to believe that a good abundant life is possible and you hunger for more. The narrow road is no longer impossible to travel on but it becomes a pleasure. You find goodness on this road to the abundant life.

As you travel this narrow road you see that the things in life that made it so difficult have less value. You learn from the mistakes of the past and it keeps you on the narrow road. You learn that there are choices that are right and there are choices that are wrong. The wrong choices become more obvious and less desirable. You want to live right. When you live right sleep is sweeter because you are making better choices and you are no longer losing sleep because of bad choices you make.

As time passes you learn more and more about this narrow road and you learn to love being on this path. Life truly does become easier and much more enjoyable than life in the world on the broad road used to be. We have a tendency as new Christians to think we have to give up so much and life can't be fun anymore. I have heard more than one person who is on the broad way who has made these claims. Oh if they could only see that their choices are many but they will lead to destruction. There are laws that God put into place that you cannot change and this one of them. Only the narrow road will lead to life.

I can still hear my dad say "Life isn't meant to be hard; we make it hard by of the choices we make." He was a very wise man and I am blessed to be his daughter. I learned a lot from him and still learn from his writings. I have also come to understand that life really is not meant to be hard, it is meant to be good and fulfilling. God has made a blessed life possible for me through Jesus Christ and I have every intention of walking on the narrow road where life is found, I hope you join me.

· KINGDOM THINKING ·

When Jesus was here on earth teaching his disciples they were thinking that He was going to overthrow Rome and build a literal kingdom here on earth at that time. They were excited about being released from the oppression of the Romans and they wanted freedom. However the kingdom that Jesus was talking about was not about overthrowing the Romans. Instead Jesus came to set up a kingdom that would teach us how to live and manage our lives according to Gods principles. The Kingdom is within us. We each govern our own bodies and choose our life's destiny based on the choices we make. Jesus came to teach us how to govern, how to think and how to live. God's Kingdom is a code of ethics to live by. There will come a time when Jesus will return and set up His literal kingdom on earth. He will reign over the entire world and we as believers will reign with Him.

2 Timothy 2:12 (NIV) *¹²If we endure, we will also reign with Him. If we disown Him, He will also disown us;*

Revelation 20:6 (NIV) *⁶Blessed and holy are those who share in the first resurrection. The second death has no power over them, but they will be priests of God and of Christ and will reign with Him for a thousand years.*

Until then He has given us a set of values or principles to live by. By instituting these values and principles into our lives we are renewing our minds to be like Christ. As we continue to learn these values and principles we are changing how we think and we are becoming a new creation. The Kingdom then lives within us. We chose now to live by these standards. These standards are not a religion but a lifestyle.

If everyone would choose to live by these standards the world around us would change. When Jesus rose from the grave there was a power shift, Satan knows there was a power shift but unfortunately we often fail to recognize it. Many Christians do not realize that they have been given this power and they just go with the flow never realizing life could be better. If we follow the value system that God set up for His Kingdom then we take dominion over our situations. As Christians we have more power than Satan does, after all the power that raised Jesus from the grave dwells in us, that is a lot of power! If we believe in the resurrection of Jesus and have accepted Him as Lord of our lives then His spirit does live in us, this quickens our mortal bodies and gives us great power.

Romans 8:11 (NIV) *11And if the Spirit of Him who raised Jesus from the dead is living in you, He who raised Christ from the dead will also give life to your mortal bodies because of his Spirit who lives in you.*

My father wrote a wonderful little booklet that talks about the Kingdom of God that will help you understand God's Kingdom. When we have Kingdom understanding life as God intended makes more sense. We have to understand what the Kingdom of God looks like in order to live our lives as God intended. I would highly recommend that you take the time to read this booklet. It is available at lared.org. Click on "church" and then "materials" there you will find free materials and several of those booklets were written by my father. The one that talks about the kingdom as called "It is Time" It will be worth your time to read all of the booklets. They are easy to read and will give you clarity on a number of topics.

4

Where Does It All Start?

Our thought life is the problem. We don't know how to think on the things of God. Our thinking has to be renewed. All of these evil things start in our minds before they become our actions. If we don't renew our thinking we will continue to follow these ungodly lifestyles. Changing our thinking is a process. We have to learn what the Word of God says then we need to meditate on it and re-read it until our spirit receives the truths and then we learn to live by these new standards.

How often do we take time to think about what we are thinking about? We go through life and quite frankly we almost never give our thoughts a thought. Our minds are filled with thoughts all day long, our minds wander and thoughts come and go without us ever realizing what is going on.

2 Corinthians 10:5 (NIV) *⁵ We demolish arguments and every pretension that sets itself up against the knowledge of God, and we take captive every thought to make it obedient to Christ.*

You cannot take every thought captive without thinking about what you are thinking about. It takes a conscience effort to take your thoughts captive. This means that you have to learn to stop and think about what you are thinking about and then learn how to change your thoughts when they do not line up with the Word of God. This will lead to other victories in your life. Take for instance the times you have said things that you shouldn't have said. If you learn to take the thoughts captive before you say them you will learn not to be so hasty in saying things. This alone will save you many embarrassing moments. You will be less likely to hurt those you love with harsh words and you'll be less likely to make a fool of yourself with your quickly spoken words.

· APPLYING IT TO YOUR LIFE ·

Several years ago I made the decision that I would learn to apply this to my life. I have learned a few things along the way and I have by no means conquered all of my thoughts but I have come a long way in learning to control my mind and taking thoughts captive and replacing them with the right thoughts. I have even learned to bite my tongue! It is amazing how many times I have caught myself before I said something. Even more amazing is how many times I have walked away from an argument without having to have the last word. I can see now that learning these things has given me great satisfaction and brought peace to my life. I am happy to let things go whether I am right or not. I do not always have to win. Even when you win in your own mind it doesn't mean you won in your opponents mind and let's face it tomorrow no one will care who won!

If you decide to take this challenge there are some things that will help you but you have to have a strong desire to accomplish it or you will never make any progress. I will share some things I did to make this a part of my life but it takes discipline and determination. I will be the first to also tell you it is a wonderful thing when you can take control of your mind. Your life will change, and you will understand how you can have peace even when things around you are in turmoil. Like I said before I haven't arrived at perfection but I am making a daily commitment to being in charge of my thoughts.

First it is important that you control the things that are going into your mind. Things like ungodly television, books and movies leave lasting images in your mind that you do not need. There is no way that you can expose yourself to the horrible language, indulgent sex, and other ungodly behavior in today's movies and TV shows without them becoming a part of your thought life. You may not say these things out loud but they are in your subconscious and very much a part of you. Once you remove these things from your life you will soon start to realize just how much of it you were putting into your mind. This is one of those disciplines that is not always easy. You get attached to your favorite TV shows and you become immune to the ungodly things that are taking place on the show. It does take determination as I mentioned earlier to be able to part with the TV; it all depends on how much desire you have to renew your mind.

Some of the scenes in movies are so ungodly and yet we expose ourselves and our children to these things and expect them not to affect our lives. Once that image is in your mind you cannot erase it. You can train your mind not to think about it but you cannot easily erase something that has been planted in your mind. Taking control of the thoughts is possible but why put yourself in the position of having to do that to begin with?

We see so much violence and adultery around us that without giving it much thought we start to think it is normal and okay, and then we expect our children to grow up knowing it is wrong. We see it on billboards throughout our cities, and even watching decent television isn't safe anymore with the commercials that are aired throughout the show. The world around us has become so corrupt and vulgar and most of us are so used to seeing it that we hardly notice what is happening all around us.

John 17:14-15 (NIV) *¹⁴I have given them your word and the world has hated them, for they are not of the world any more than I am of the world. ¹⁵My prayer is not that you take them out of the world but that you protect them from the evil one.*

This scripture is part of prayer that Jesus prayed for us while He was here on the earth. This prayer that Jesus prayed over us is so precious and gives us a picture of the heart of Christ. I would highly recommend that you spend some time reading through John seventeen and even fifteen and sixteen. These are some of my favorite chapters in the Bible. Jesus understood that we will be faced with many difficult things and He is praying that we will be protected from the evil one. We can do a lot to help with this by removing the ungodly things from our lives. The evil one loves to slip things in under our noses in hopes that we don't recognize his ways. He is sly and he does not give up easily but you can learn to see him for what he is. Remember he is out to destroy you.

God isn't asking to do something that cannot be done. We live in this world but we do not have to be a part of the things the world is doing. We have the choice to be in control of our lives and things we surround ourselves with.

· WORRY ·

There are many other areas where we can apply the idea of taking our thoughts captive. Let's start by looking at worry.

When we worry, we are not taking our thoughts captive. We allow our mind to go anywhere it chooses to go, which is why we are worried to begin with. If you take those thoughts captive and refuse to give in to them you can sleep and be at peace. Worry isn't going to change anything about your situation, it isn't going to solve any problems and it certainly isn't going to change anyone. Worry is a waste of time! I can look back on my life and see that I have lost several years worth of sleep worrying about things that never happened or things that I had no control over to begin with. What a waste of time!

There are people who are actually known as worriers. Who in their right mind would want that reputation? Take those thoughts captive and live in peace. Understand the truth about worry and be set free.

Matthew 6:27 (NIV) *27Can any one of you by worrying add a single hour to your life?*

Isn't that amazing, all that worrying that you have done has not added even one hour to your life. Actually I believe worry will shorten your life, it is unhealthy!

· SELFISHNESS ·

Selfishness is another big problem we all face. It is nothing more than thinking of ourselves, filling our minds with thoughts of "me". We can spend so much time thinking of ourselves that we don't see the needs of others in our world. This type of thinking has to change. The world is not all about me and my thought life shouldn't be either. I can take these thoughts captive and learn to think differently. When you catch yourself all caught up in selfish thoughts become aware of it and start thinking about what you can do for someone else, then step out in action to meet the needs of someone else.

If you have been doing everything for yourself and not for others they may not know how to respond to the new you. Chances are pretty good that they would be suspicious and wonder how long can the new you last?

The really good news to all of this is that you will be the one that benefits the most! It's kind of like the principle of giving away and receiving more in return than you gave away. The Kingdom of God can sometimes feel a bit upside down. What we need to remember is that God is the creator so His way is the right way and is not the upside version. We as humans have taken the right way and turned it upside down so for us it is truly a new way of thinking but it is the right way!

This reminds me of a song we used to sing about a magic penny. The song says "Love is something if you give it away, you'll end up having more. It's just like a magic penny, lend it spend it you'll have so many they'll roll all over the floor." You cannot out give God and love conquers all things!

There are many people who would claim that they are not selfish however when you take a real look at what selfishness is you will find that we have all been selfish. When we talk about changing our thinking it is not a small thing. We have to learn to put the needs of others ahead of our own. Do unto others as you would have them do unto you, is a Biblical principle. If we would all just start with this one little thing the world would greatly improve immediately. Just imagine a world where everyone would be doing what is right for the other person without giving a thought to themselves and their own wants and desires. Think about how that would look in your own life.

Selfishness would disappear. Not only would you treat others differently they would also put you ahead of their own needs. If your neighbor was in need, you would be the solution. Most of us probably don't even know our neighbors much less know what their needs are. Some of our children wouldn't know how to respond to a parent who is paying attention to them and putting them ahead of themselves. People would let you make a left turn in front of them and you would allow people to cross the street while you wait patiently. The way things are now few people are considerate or patient enough to allow anyone to cross the street in front of them. And if by chance someone is brave enough to step out in front of us we will do all we can to make it look like we almost hit them, lets teach them a lesson is often our attitude. Little acts of kindness cost us nothing but gain us the world. People do appreciate being treated nicely and who knows your example may cause them to do the same for someone else. An act of kindness will often be passed on to the next person. An act of kindness brings a great feeling of satisfaction.

One little principle when followed by everyone would change the whole world and how we see each other. But let's face it, not everyone is going to make this change. So how would it look if just you made this change, "Do unto others as you would have them do unto you?"

How would your home be different? Would your children notice, would your spouse notice? How would your workplace be different? Whose respect would you gain? Who would you inspire?

When you stop being selfish and start treating others the way you want to be treated you will be amazed at the satisfaction you get from following just this one principle. You start feeling better about yourself as well as the people around you. You'll find that some of the very people who bothered you the most will turn out to be some the nicest people you know. When you are kind, others tend to be kind as well. It may take some of them some time but they will change when you change and no matter how long it takes for them to change they will not bother you nearly as much as they did in the past because your attitude towards them has changed. That is called a new way of thinking, and you are going to like how it feels!

If you have children at home this is a great thing to teach them while they are young. When you take time to instill these simple yet profound truths in your children you are making a great investment into their futures. When a child can grow up with the right thinking he will never have to learn to take some of these thoughts captive and learn how to think properly. He will still face enough other ways of thinking that he will have to change but you will have helped him have a better outlook on life from a young age. You are only one person but your change in this area can affect many others and one by one we can teach the world how to be respectful of each other, treating them the way we want to be treated.

The next time you get irritated at someone take your thoughts captive and re-evaluate the situation. How would you handle this if you put the other person first and treated them the way you would want to be treated in the same situation? I didn't say to treat them as they deserved, but how you would want to be treated. If we were always treated the way we deserve I doubt that life would feel great for any of us.

· JUDGMENT ·

How often do you think that you misjudge a situation then respond to the person according to the way you have judged? It happens all the time. Remember that the other person has a story. You have no idea what they have been through; you do not know what happened this morning in their life. If you can remember that, then you will learn to treat others with more respect. No matter what their morning or your morning was like there is no reason not to treat them with respect. Why not think the best of others rather than assuming the worst?

None of this is our nature; we react and judge without thinking many times. We judge others by what we see not by what we know. When we do think we know something about the person we may not have the truth about them. We can judge a person by what we think is the truth but thinking and knowing are two different things. They are just as human as we are. I know this may be a new idea to you but really they are no different than you are. We have all been guilty of treating others by the way they act or talk or by the way they are treating us. If they don't know Jesus you can't blame them for what they do not know. Quite possibly when you reflect Jesus they will see that you are different, they may see the light and have a desire to change. Sometimes when someone makes a big change others want to know what has happened to cause the change. It opens doors to share the gospel of Jesus with others and that is our mission! We are called to go into the world and make disciples. (Matthew 28:19) Others judge us by what they see and by how we act and I bet that doesn't always look very good.

We all have people in our lives that we would say "rub us the wrong way". There is something about them that we don't like and we may not even know exactly what it is but we just know we don't really want to be around them. I believe that this often happens when we don't know a person well. We have predetermined (judged) what type of person they are by what others have said or by the person's behavior. However how many times are we having a bad day and we carry it with us throughout the day and we ourselves rub others the wrong way? Others see us when we are not in the best spirits and they decide that we are moody or unfriendly when we were just having a bad day. If we are having a bad day maybe we should consider starting the next day with God in some quiet time, it can make a world of difference.

We judge in this way all the time. We are guilty. We can make excuses and say "we are only human" which is obvious but is that really a good excuse? We don't want others to judge us yet we do it to them all the time. So how do we remedy this and how do we capture our judgmental thoughts and trade them in for good thoughts towards other people?

We have to be aware of our thoughts when we start judging others. The more you practice this the easier it becomes. Perfection in this is hard, I know because I have been working on this for quite a while. I am getting better at it but I still catch myself with judgmental thoughts I should not have. I am constantly becoming more aware and I am making progress slow but sure.

· FEAR ·

I think fear is one of the hardest things to change in our thought life. Some people are so fearful they do not trust anyone. They are constantly looking for bad things to happen in their lives. Others are afraid of being alone or afraid of the future. People fear all kinds of things. Fear can be overcome.

We need to stop and remind ourselves that we are never alone. The Holy Spirit is always with us and God said He would never leave us.

Isaiah 41:10 (NIV)

¹⁰So do not fear, for I am with you;
    do not be dismayed, for I am your God.

I will strengthen you and help you;
    I will uphold you with My righteous right hand.

We allow our minds to rest on the things we fear and they grow bigger and bigger the more time we spend there. We need to replace thoughts of fear with the goodness of God. God's goodness and love and mercy far outweigh any fear that we may have. Learning to trust God is a big part in overcoming this situation and many others in your life. Remembering Gods teaching promises you peace and prosperity.

Proverbs 3:3-6 (NIV)

3My son, do not forget my teaching,
    but keep My commands in your heart,
2for they will prolong your life many years
    and bring you peace and prosperity.
3Let love and faithfulness never leave you;
    bind them around your neck,
    write them on the tablet of your heart.
4Then you will win favor and a good name
    in the sight of God and man.
5Trust in the Lord with all your heart
    and lean not on your own understanding;
6in all your ways submit to Him,
    and He will make your paths straight.

Keep your mind focused on God and fear will leave you, take those thoughts captive and trade them in for the scriptures above, memorize them and use them often.

· WHO WE ARE IN CHRIST ·

First we need to remember who we are in Christ and determine that we can live a better life. We are not living our lives for ourselves but as ambassadors for Christ. Can the people around us see that we are Christians? Could we be proven to be Christians, is there evidence of it? Or are we living like the world around us hiding our faith and trying to live a privately Christian life? If we are guilty of judging others, condemning them for their behavior, or allowing our "bad day" to shine, we are definitely not taking our thoughts captive. This type of behavior is what brought us to the end of ourselves to begin with, why would we want to return to that old way of life?

Let's talk about the bad day we tend to have on occasion. We only have bad days if we do not take our thoughts captive. For an example, your frame of mind is what determines your day. If your mind is wrapped around having a bad day and you confess a bad day with your mouth you are setting yourself up for a bad day. Now if you take that thought captive and you remind yourself that you are a child of God, and you walk in victory by faith not by sight you can change the thought process and have a good day. Throughout the day you may have to remind yourself of these truths but it can be done.

Proverbs 23:3 (NIV) *As a man thinks in his heart so is he.*

That is pretty self explanatory. You are the way you think and your day will be according to how you think. Taking those negative thoughts captive and changing the negative thoughts to positive thoughts will change the outcome of your day. This means that you have to take control. You cannot let your natural mind go wherever it wants to go. Take the thought captive then confess it with your mouth. Say it out loud, "I am going to have a great day because I am a child of God." Fight against those negative thoughts and it will become a way of life.

Most of us have been around people who seem to always be

on top of things. They do not appear to ever struggle through a bad day and they are always happy. Those are the people who have taken their thoughts captive and they think on the good things in life. That can be you, it can be me. It is as simple as a choice!

Sometimes people are known as mean spirited people. When you are around them there is heaviness in the air. It is downright depressing and you just want to get away. These people seldom have friends because no one wants to be around a person like that. Maybe that person is you. The good news is this pattern can be changed and this person can become new. That is what salvation and a new way of thinking can do. Everyone can change; there is hope for everyone you know. You can change your life but you cannot change the other person. A change in your life can influence another person and your change can become infectious. You can be an inspiration to those around you, a new you can speak very loudly to those people who are a part of your life. Taking thoughts captive is the first step to living a victorious life.

5

Take Every Thought Captive

Just how do you take your thoughts captive? How do you learn to stop before you react and say things you'll regret later? How do you become this new person with a new way of thinking? Our actions are thoughts first. They come from inside of us, from what is in our hearts.

In Mark chapter seven we read where Jesus was talking to the Pharisees and the teachers of the law. They had a lot of hang ups about following unwritten laws. They were following these laws for many years and they became their religion. To them not following them was sin and unlawful. They condemned Jesus followers for not washing their hands, in the ceremonial way of the unwritten law, before they ate. They were more concerned about proper washing of hands than they were of the thoughts and the evil in their hearts. Jesus accused them of ignoring the commands of God so that they could follow their own laws. These people were blind and didn't understand. In verse seventeen we see that the disciples didn't understand what Jesus was talking about either so Jesus explained it to them.

Mark 7:20-23 (NIV) *20He went on: "What comes out of a person is what defiles them. 21For it is from within, out of a person's heart, that evil thoughts come—sexual immorality, theft, murder, 22adultery, greed, malice, deceit, lewdness, envy, slander, arrogance and folly. 23All these evils come from inside and defile a person."*

Knowing that what we do starts with what we think, should give us good reason to take our thoughts captive. That thought will eventually become an action.

Our thinking matters and we have to guard our hearts and learn that our thoughts can be controlled. I learned about controlling my thoughts during a very hard time in my life.

One of the worst things that ever happened in my life was so devastating that I wasn't sure I could live through it. The pain of it was so great I could hardly make myself get out of bed in the mornings. All day every day my thoughts held me captive. I played scenes over and over in my mind till I almost drove myself crazy. For three months I basically ceased to exist. I was numb with pain and really did not want to live one more day. It took me years to get beyond the pain and really be able to move past it. I had nightmares that kept me awake at night and afraid to go back to sleep. I cried more tears than I thought a human had. I survived, but that was about all.

I finally got to the point that I was able to realize that all the pictures I was allowing to play over and over in my mind were hurting me. They didn't solve anything but they made things much worse. Somehow I had to learn to remove the pictures in my mind and replace them with new ones; I had to take my thoughts captive if I wanted to have a normal life again.

It was during this time that I first learned that you can take thoughts captive. It took me many more years to realize that I could take other thoughts captive as well and change how I thought. I started this process after I had pretty much come to the end of myself and decided to try to live again. Little by little I started painting new images in my mind. When a negative picture came into my mind I would try to catch it before I lingered there and replace it with something else. I had to put a lot of effort into finding new pictures to replace the ones I had been thinking about for so long. I would find one good thing to think about and use it over and over till I came up with another one I could use. I cannot tell you how difficult this was but because I decided that I wanted to move on and start living again I put forth the effort it took.

Over a period of several years I was finally able to think about other things. I remember well when the first day passed and I realized at the end of the day I had gone a whole day without those damaging pictures going through my head. Day after day I made progress. Finally a week went by and then a month, I started to live again. I remember the day that my dad said to me "it is so nice to hear you laugh again." Until he said that I was not even aware that I had not laughed for a long time. That has been more than twenty five years ago and today I am happy, I laugh and enjoy life. This is possible for anyone who has been deeply wounded. For the change to occur and for life to begin again you have to make the choice to start living again, you will have to develop new pictures in your mind to think on.

If I allow myself I can still see the pictures and feel the pain of it. There are some things in life that are so life changing and devastating that you can always remember the pain. But you don't have to think on those things! Allowing yourself to relive these horrible events is damaging no one but you. The choice becomes ours, do we want to live it again or do we want to move on? If we are not careful, living in that pain can become who we are. If we chose not to move beyond it, it becomes a permanent part of us and we become known for the depression we have chosen to live in. Life will never be happy till we decide to move on and leave the pain in the past.

If you have buried yourself in past pain that you cannot seem to move out of, I want you to know you can move on and you can choose to forget it. When I realized that I was only hurting myself and making things worse by always thinking about this I decided it is not how I wanted to live the rest of my life. I made a conscience effort to think differently.

We all have things that our minds want to go to, thoughts that are not beneficial. These thoughts can destroy our lives if we let them. We have to choose intentionally to change things that we can change and then our thought pattern can change.

When we purpose to change the thoughts in our heads it can be a challenge. We have been thinking the same way for many years. Often we are not even aware of how awful our thoughts have become, or how judgmental we are. It feels normal to be the way we are and changing from what feels normal is not easy.

Decide on one thought pattern you have that you want to change and work on just that one thing. For instance if you are selfish as we talked about earlier, realize it and learn to catch those selfish thoughts and replace them with something good.

Philippians 4:8 (NIV) *8Finally, brothers and sisters, whatever is true, whatever is noble, whatever is right, whatever is pure, whatever is lovely, whatever is admirable—if anything is excellent or praiseworthy—think about such things.*

In my example above I had to find something good to think

about, I purposely found a new picture, a new image and used it. To change your selfish thoughts you need to do the same thing. In the scripture above are several ideas as to where you can choose to take your thoughts. Let's take the idea of thinking on something that is true and find something we can have ready to replace those selfish thoughts and habits.

Proverbs 11:24-25 (NIV)

²⁴One person gives freely, yet gains even more;
*   another withholds unduly, but comes to poverty.*
²⁵A generous person will prosper;
*   whoever refreshes others will be refreshed.*

Now that is something for a selfish person to think on! I said earlier that the Kingdom of God seems upside down but knowing that God is God and we are not makes it evident that we need to believe this truth. Gods truths always work and the sooner we realize that and put them into practice in our lives the sooner we will live that abundant life. Selfishness hurts us as well as the other person. When we give away whether it is time, money, compliments or kindness we always gain more in return for ourselves.

When you find yourself being selfish, catch the thought and trade it in for the one above. In time you will find yourself changing, and believing what the Word of God says.

Philippians 2:3-4 (NIV)

³Do nothing out of selfish ambition or vain conceit. Rather, in humility value others above yourselves, ⁴not looking to your own interests but each of you to the interests of the others.

There it is again, think of others, treat them the way you want to be treated.

It is amazing that we tend to categorize sins into different categories of how bad they are. We tend to think that selfishness is not as bad as adultery but look at what the Word of God tells us.

Galatians 5:19-21 (NIV) *19 The acts of the flesh are obvious: sexual immorality, impurity and debauchery; 20idolatry and witchcraft; hatred, discord, jealousy, fits of rage, selfish ambition, dissensions, factions 21 and envy; drunkenness, orgies, and the like. I warn you, as I did before, that those who live like this will not inherit the kingdom of God.*

Ouch, that hurts! However we need to learn the truth and then live by what we have learned. This does not paint a very pretty picture of selfishness. If you want to inherit the Kingdom of God you need to change your selfish ways and think of others more highly than yourself.

Once you get into this habit you will learn to like yourself a bit better. You cannot live against the Word of God and really feel good about yourself. God created us for a higher purpose. We are often limited because of sin in our lives. We may tend to be jealous or selfish we may be a gossip or a trouble maker and any of these things will limit our effectiveness as Christians. When we learn that these things are inside of us and they are displeasing to God we can make changes in these areas of our lives by being aware of our thoughts and we can become more Christ like. God wants to work all those ungodly traits out of our lives so that we can show the world what true Christianity looks like. It is always easier for us to see these sins in other people than in our own lives, but let's step back and take a closer look at our own behavior, our own habits and our own ungodly thoughts and determine to change, by renewing our minds.

Matthew 7:3 (NIV) *3 "Why do you look at the speck of sawdust in your brother's eye and pay no attention to the plank in your own eye?*

Before we can help others we need to see who we are and change the things that God shows us we need to change. Let's remove the stumbling blocks that trip us up before we try to help others. This is an ongoing process and will take us a lifetime. As we see one problem in our lives and work to correct it another one will be made clear and we start on that problem area. It's called growth.

· GOD HAS A PURPOSE FOR YOUR LIFE ·

I think as a Christian we all want to fulfill God's call on our lives. There is something within us that tells us we were created for more. Unless we resolve to walk in what God has for us, life will pass us by and we will never see the good things God has in store for us. Sometimes we are so heavenly minded that we forget that the abundant life promised to us was for this life not the next one. We already know that heaven will be beyond anything we can imagine but we are currently not living in heaven. Right now, right here we have a life to live. This is the life that gives us choices; this is the life that allows us to decide how to live. In heaven there are no choices that involve sin and living right. Only now can we live is such a way that others will want what we have.

All around us, every day there are people who are lost, people who are searching for answers, we have the answers if we are Christ's followers. Get into the Word so that you can lead others to Christ. How awful to be in a place where you could have the chance to witness and lead someone to Christ and then not know for sure what God's Word says. We have many lost opportunities because of our lack of understanding.

What are your priorities? How important is an abundant life? Can you imagine getting to heaven and then discovering all that could have been a part of your life here on earth and all that you missed because you were a lazy Christian? Sometimes we hear the phrase "what if you are the only Christian someone will ever see" I say "you are the only Christian some people will ever see". Each one of us makes a difference either for good or…

6

Facing Trials

· THINK IT NOT STRANGE THAT
FIERY TRIAL THAT COMES UPON YOU ·

We all face trials, but we don't all handle them the same. A trial is never fun but they are always an opportunity to learn something new. Sometimes when I am going through a difficult time I will pray that God will help me learn this lesson so that I can move on to something else. Let's face it, it is just no fun! Have you noticed that you get to face the same trial over and over again, it is a sure sign that you have not yet learned the lesson the trial was meant to teach. Sometimes we don't even think of it as a trial that can teach us something instead we look at it as a general problem we have and not as something we can overcome. Maybe you think it's everybody else's fault, if so maybe it's time to look in the mirror and ask yourself if you are the problem and just maybe it is time to overcome?

One of my favorite books in the Bible is the book of James. I was in a church service one time when our pastor mentioned that he had memorized the book of James and I decided that if he could do that then so could I. What a wonderful experience that became. I fell in love with the book of James and have often gone back to it just to reread it and think on all the treasures it contains. The book of James has so much to offer us when we want to change how we think. We learn to look at things differently and it changes our behavior and our thinking.

James 1:2-8 (NIV) *²Consider it pure joy, my brothers and sisters, whenever you face trials of many kinds, ³because you know that the testing of your faith produces perseverance. ⁴Let perseverance finish its work so that you may be mature and complete, not lacking anything. ⁵If any of you lacks wisdom, you should ask God, who gives generously to all without finding fault, and it will be given to you. ⁶But when you ask, you must believe and not doubt, because the one who doubts is like a wave of the sea, blown and tossed by the wind. ⁷That person should not expect to receive anything from the Lord. ⁸Such a person is double-minded and unstable in all they do.*

Wow there is so much in these verses that we need to take a look at. Not too many of us ever consider it pure joy when we face a trial. That is not our human nature. We cry the blues and feel sorry for ourselves maybe we even tell everyone around us how unfair life is. But the truth is the trial, when handled correctly produces perseverance. I have lived long enough to know that perseverance is something I need to be able to get through things that happen in life.

When a trial comes it takes faith to get through it. We cannot always see what the outcome will be and sometimes the trial takes much longer than we naturally have the patience for. We want solutions quickly, we live in a world of instant everything and trials just are not an instant fix. There is much to be learned in trials.

It takes wisdom to learn from the trial and to apply the truth to our situation. This verse tells us we can ask God for wisdom and he will give it to us, but it also says that we cannot be double minded and expect anything from the Lord. Sometimes I think I am not double minded and I am sure you have done the same thing. Let me ask you a question "Have you ever put into words a negative comment about a situation you are going through?" In other words when we are praying for an answer and we believe that the answer will come but then we say things like "It is never going to happen." or "Things just don't change" that is being double minded. You pray and ask for one thing but you confess another thing when you talk to your friends and family. If that is what we are doing then we shouldn't expect an answer. That is being double minded and James tells us if we are double minded we shouldn't expect to receive anything from the Lord.

It takes wisdom to see and make these changes in our lives, wisdom that we do not have in and of ourselves, but wisdom that comes from God. We are to ask God for wisdom and we are told that He will give it to us if we do not doubt.

We are going to the beach on a family vacation in a few weeks. I love to watch the ocean, see the waves as they crash against the shore. These waves are blown and tossed by the wind. The wind in the ocean can be a wild thing. Recently we were on a cruise when the wind became rough and it blew the ship around till the swimming pool was nearly empty by morning. That is how our unbelief looks to God. We are tossed around like a wave in the wind and unstable in all that we do! We should not think we will receive anything from the Lord. (vs. 7 & 8)

I strongly believe that our words have lots of power and when we continue to confess with our mouths negative outcomes and negative thoughts we put what we say into effect. We need to learn to confess the right answer and then pray expecting the right outcome. The words you speak have power and will produce fruit.

Proverbs 18:21 (NIV)

21 The tongue has the power of life and death,
  and those who love it will eat its fruit.

Some of the trials I have faced were the result of my asking God to purify me. I want to be purified but I don't like the process, because it is painful. The trial comes when God shows me what needs to change in my life. Recently I again prayed that prayer and God showed me a flaw in my character I had no idea was there. I was shocked to realize it. I see in myself something that needs to change and I cannot say that I feel confident that I can do it; at least I know I cannot do it without the help of the Holy Spirit. It is something I want to change because I know the change would please God and it would greatly change my life. The trial is in my head. I have to change how I see certain things, I have to find within me the courage to make the change if I want God to use me the way I know God wants to use me. I do want to be used by God and I want to fulfill what God created for me to do and I see that until I can make this change and accept how it will affect my life I am at a standstill.

My biggest obstacle is getting over what others would think, how will I be thought of by others; will I make a fool of myself by stepping out and being vulnerable? I shouldn't even think about what others will think I should care only what God thinks. Why are we so hung up on the opinion of others and what they think of us? I know my life will be more fulfilled and I will have a greater impact on the world for Christ when I accept this challenge and take the leap of faith it requires.

Taking the leap of faith is a big challenge. I think of my young granddaughter when I think of taking this leap. She was about two years old and at the family pool with her daddy. He stood in the pool encouraging her to jump into the water, assuring her that he would catch her. You could see in her excitement and hear it in her giggle that she wanted to jump, but she was afraid to take the leap. She would get down ready to jump then giggle and back away from the pool; she had done it before and knew it would be a great experience but fear still kept her from making the jump.

As I watched her I could see the anticipation. She wanted to do it. She knew it was the right thing to do and she even saw others doing it but when it came down to it, she was afraid her daddy wouldn't catch her. It dawned on me that the joy was in the jump, without the jump or leap of faith there was only a nervous anticipation. That is how I feel right now. I know it is the right thing to do, I know I heard from God but I cannot say that I am without some fear of what it might look like in my life and then there is the trust issue. Do I really trust God to be with me and not let me fall? Until I take the leap I am in the trial. It will bother me because I know I need to go for it.

How am I handling this? The first thing I did was ask God to forgive me for my shortsightedness. How could I not recognize this in myself? I have asked the Holy Spirit to help me because this is way beyond my comfort zone and without Him I will never do it. I actually thought I had this one, I thought I understood and that this particular thing wasn't working in my life for a far different reason than I now understand. I have to say I was shocked to hear this from the Lord.

I think we are all supposed to be out of our comfort zone. As long as we stay in our comfort zone the impact we have for

Christ is limited. God wants us to be totally dependent on Him doing things we can only do through Him. We will then be in a position that we cannot take the credit, all the glory will go to the Father.

I want to be mature and complete not lacking anything. That is a big statement. I think that sometimes we tend to think of ourselves more highly than we ought and we think we are doing all we can for Christ but we are limiting Him because we take the credit for ourselves. If we aren't doing the things that are beyond us, the things that we can only do through Christ and the Holy Spirit then we are not doing the right things, the things that will make the biggest difference in our lives as well as in the lives of others are the things we cannot do on our own.

This is only one trial in my life but I have others as well. I know this one will last as long as it takes me to take that leap and even then I doubt that will be the end of the thing. I will fail at times and I will look foolish at times but I will be in step with what the Lord has told me to do, making the change that he has shown me to make.

Our lives are to make a difference in the world. Somehow we get comfortable and want to make the impact inside the four walls of the church. If we look at the life of Christ most of his ministry was in the marketplace. People were amazed by the miracles and it drew them to Christ and He taught them the ways of God. We are more comfortable working our ministry in the church than in the marketplace.

I believe that the church will undergo some changes and that we are called to go to the marketplace and let the world see Christ in us. Too many Christians have the attitude that church and Christianity are a separate issue from everyday life. We go to church and hear about the Kingdom of God but then leave the service thinking the Kingdom of God is inside the church. What we need to realize is that the Kingdom of God is in us and we are the church, the bride of Christ. We carry the Kingdom of God with us and we are to make an impact on the world.

When you realize that the Kingdom of God is within you, it's a new way of thinking, this means the Kingdom of God is a part of everyday life. You act and react differently. You talk differently and think differently. The Kingdom within you becomes a very real part of your life every day. You grow and mature as you gain new understanding of this Kingdom and it just overflows. People start to see that you are different from others they know; you want to be purified and have more understanding and knowledge about God. You want to learn and live by this new way.

Not everyone is asking God for purification, I know it can be a dangerous thing to ask for but I want to do what God wants me to do and in order to do that I need to ask for more. I don't want to stop learning or growing in the Lord. I want everything He has for me even when it is out of my comfort zone so I ask for purification. God loves me enough not to show me more than I can handle at any time. Now I am being encouraged to take the leap and God knows just where to give me the nudge and make me go for it. I am sure there is much more to learn after this.

We face lots of trials without asking for purification. Our children become a trial at times. You teach them what is right and as adults they still make the wrong choice. You carry the burden and it becomes a trial. There is a coworker who makes your life miserable and you go to work each day facing a trial. We face sickness and death, life is full of trials. God has told us that the faith it takes to get through all of these things develops perseverance and it's the perseverance that brings maturity and completes us.

James 1:12 (NIV) *12Blessed is the one who perseveres under trial because, having stood the test, that person will receive the crown of life that the Lord has promised to those who love Him.*

Don't you just love God's promises? I want that crown of life. I want to live a life that I will be happy to answer for when I stand before God at the second coming.

There is a difference between testing and tempting. God does not tempt anyone. Temptation to do evil is always from Satan. Falling for temptation always brings destruction but testing in trials and persevering always brings a better life. Temptation does not bring about maturity, but ends in defeat. The temptation is the first step to disaster that is why you have to take that thought captive (2 Corinthians 10:5) and understand where it comes from. If you allow the thought it will become an action and the action will bring death when it is full grown. Testing brings maturity, temptation when followed brings death.

James 1:13-15 (NIV) *13When tempted, no one should say, "God is tempting me." For God cannot be tempted by evil, nor does he tempt anyone; 14but each person is tempted when they are dragged away by their own evil desire and enticed. 15Then, after desire has conceived, it gives birth to sin; and sin, when it is full-grown, gives birth to death.*

When Satan tempts us we need to stand strong and take our thoughts captive. We need to change our thinking and not fall into his traps.

I loved listening to a Sunday school teacher recently who described this temptation as bait. Satan puts out the bait and if we are not careful we go for the bait and then the trap snaps and we are caught up in sin. We need to be aware of the bait and understand who it is that has put out the bait. If you don't go for the bait the trap cannot get you.

We had a raccoon problem this past winter. One of our buildings is in a wooded area and not used during the winter months. I had asked our repairman to keep an eye on the building, checking it out about once a week during the winter months. One day he came to the office and told me an animal had broken through the overhang of the building and been inside destroying some of the things that were stored in it. He wasn't sure what the animal was but we knew we had to trap it or it would just come back and do more damage. We were not sure if the animal was still inside the building or not so we set two live traps, one inside the building and one outside. We repaired the hole it had made to get inside and then waited to see what we would catch. After two days we had caught nothing inside the building but the bait from the trap outside had been taken, but no animal was caught in the trap. New bait was put out but again the animal outsmarted us and got away with the bait. My repairman decided to use cat food instead of the apple that the pest control people were using. The next morning we had trapped a rather large raccoon. When the first bait didn't work the new bait did and we caught the predator.

I think Satan works the same way. He will try to get you off track with one tactic and when that doesn't ensnare you he will try something else. Until we realize that we have more power than he does we can easily fall for the trap he has set for us. We need to be wise and alert. We know what are weaknesses are so we need to protect ourselves and not put ourselves at risk where we know we may be weak. We need to use the name of Jesus and command Satan to leave. Many of the trials we face are there because we yield to the temptations of Satan.

We need to realize that the God we serve is faithful, always faithful and He does not change. We can count on him to help us through any trials that come our way. He will help keep us safe from the traps that are set to ensnare us, He is a good God.

All good things come from above from our Savior who does not change like shifting shadows.

James 1:17 *¹⁷Every good and perfect gift is from above, coming down from the Father of the heavenly lights, who does not change like shifting shadows.*

One of the things that I hear Christians saying at times is that God put a sickness on them or a loved one to teach them something. What kind of a father would do that? In James we read that all good things come from above, from a God that does not change like shifting shadows. God does not put sickness on anyone! There is nowhere in the New Testament that you can read that Jesus made anyone sick to teach them something. He came to heal and deliver the sick and oppressed.

Matthew 7:9-11 (NIV) *⁹Which of you, if your son asks for bread, will give him a stone? ¹⁰Or if he asks for a fish, will give him a snake? ¹¹If you, then, though you are evil, know how to give good gifts to your children, how much more will your Father in heaven give good gifts to those who ask Him!*

God is good, He is kind and loving. No loving father would wish sickness on his child to teach them a lesson. We will face trials and tests but they are to develop us not to destroy us. Only Satan is out to destroy you, he is the roaming the earth looking for someone to devour.

1 Peter 5:8 (NIV) *⁸Be alert and of sober mind. Your enemy the devil prowls around like a roaring lion looking for someone to devour.*

Recognize where temptation and all other things such as sickness and discouragement come from and then take authority over it. You have that power; it has been given to you by the Holy Spirit. We fail to use the power we have been given and become victims of the enemy. Our lives aren't blessed because we don't take what has been given to us; Jesus provided everything we need to live a life of power over the devil. Satan has been defeated but he wants you to believe otherwise. Don't be fooled, even he knows that he is defeated. Too often we just allow his lies to penetrate our lives and we live as though we are defeated too.

This again brings me back to Romans 12:2 where we are told to be transformed by a new way of thinking. You need to remind yourself of who you are in Christ and remind the devil that he has no power over you. The only time he has any power over you is when you believe that he does and you fall for his lies. Stop this kind of thinking, it is destroying your life. Remember that the devil will tempt you but God never tempts anyone. When you are tempted to do wrong stop and realize whose voice you are listening to.

For many people the idea of changing how they think has never been considered. They allow their minds to wander aimlessly and just assume they have no power to change their thoughts. So they live this life drifting with no real purpose or value for helping others change because their own lives are such a mess. Life is more than that! There is no abundance of good living in this type of lifestyle.

While God does not tempt us with evil we will face trials. Life is not without struggles. Every trial in life can be lived through and there is always something wonderful you will learn from any trial you go through. It is in trials that my life with Christ became more real. When I could see that I alone couldn't fix the problem and I had to learn to lean on God that my relationship with God became real. Now I don't think twice when I face a trial, I go directly to God and hand it to Him, knowing that I cannot deal with it on my own. It doesn't mean that I don't at times let my mind get the best of me and try to fix it on my own but I have learned to recognize the tricks of the enemy and I stop myself before I allow it to consume me.

There is nothing new under the sun, someone somewhere has gone through whatever you are going through, they survived and so will you. However the end of the trial is not always the same for every person. Some people come out the other side of a trial on fire for God and others seem to barely come out alive. It is all in how you look at the trial, how you handle the situation and to whom you look to for help.

We all know people who have come out of trials in one of these two ways. They have both lived through similar trials, but the outcome has been very different. When you face a trial decide how you will come out of it, what will you have done to make sure that you come out on top? If you feel sorry for yourself, have a pity me party, and walk around with a sad face telling everyone how hard life is you have opened the door to a disastrous ending to your trial. Your words will bring forth the life that you have confessed.

On the other hand you can put a smile on your face and walk with a spring in your step because you know where your help comes from. You understand you are not alone and that you are going to learn something valuable through this and you will walk in victory. You are taking your thoughts captive; you are not allowing defeat and gloom to govern your life. You are thinking and talking positively about the situation knowing that God has this one. Learn from the trial and then you will be able to help someone else when they face a similar situation.

There are many people who struggle because they are consumed with what other people are saying or thinking of them. This becomes a trial and we don't often see it as a trial. If you have a tendency to be one of these people who loses sleep because of what is being said, let me assure you that if anyone is talking about you or your family because of problems you are facing, they will soon be talking about someone else's problems. You have to learn not to care. There will always be people who want things to talk about but rest assured no matter what you are going through the whole world does not know about it. I have been through enough things with my family to give people lots to talk about but I know it will be short lived and they will soon find someone else who they will consider has more interesting issues than I do. Quite frankly I don't care if they talk! They will have family issues at some point because no one has a perfect family; no one has a perfect life. Let it go, it is not worth losing sleep over someone else's over active mouth. Don't let them become a trial for you.

In "Change Begins with Me" one of my previous books, I talked about the trial I have gone through with a prodigal son. I love my son and I want him to have a good life. He has made some really bad choices and I am waiting for him to turn his life around and live for Christ. I stand on promises in the Bible and I have full confidence that it will turn around and all will be well. That does not mean there are not consequences for bad choices that have been made but there is still a life of victory for him when he comes to repentance. Sometimes when we have made bad choices it looks so daunting. We can realize that we have gone down the wrong path and we know we have to turn around but we see how much time we have lost and it can be overwhelming. But with God it is never too late to have a good life. God can take any life that is submitted to Him and use it to advance the Kingdom. Never give up on having a good life. God is the author of good things and that includes your life as well as the lives of your children.

There have been several occasions where I have had confirmation that this will all turn out all right. It has however been several years since I have had clear confirmation but that does not get me off track. I believe God and it does not matter how it looks in the natural, I know what I know. Early in this journey I went to God a lot and I needed to know that He was in this with me, I didn't want to go it alone. I had several confirmations along the way that helped me to endure. Now it has been a number of years but I have matured in the process and although I love signs and hearing from God on this matter I don't have to have them. God has spoken and I have heard; now I trust.

I travel some and one time early during this trial I was at an airport waiting to board a plane for Florida. Before boarding began I asked God to give me an interesting seat partner, one that I would know He sent for me. I had never asked this of God before but I felt that I would hear from God on this flight. I boarded before the person beside me and anxiously waited to see who God would be sending my way. After a few minutes a young man who was obviously gay stopped and looked at his ticket and confirmed that he had the right seat. He sat down and I thought to myself "well maybe not today God". Oh how we judge from the surface! Shame on me! He sat down and we said a brief hi and I decided I would just read my book and mind my own business. I picked up my book and started looking at it when he leaned over and asked "What are you reading?" Again I had my own thoughts, "Oh this should be good" I told him I was reading a book about the Holy Spirit. He smiled and I continued to page through the book. "Is it any good?" he asked. I explained to him that I hadn't read any of it yet but that I expected it to be good since I had read another book by the same author.

He again sat back in his seat, and a few seconds later he leaned over and asked "Are you searching for something?" This time I decided to take time and talk to this fellow. I told him about my prodigal son, and I told him I am looking for answers, I talked for a few minutes not looking at him but explaining the situation to him and that I believed that God would bring my prodigal home. When I finished talking I looked over at him and he had big tears in his eyes and he said "I am a prodigal son." He then told me his story. He had grown up in a good home and then as a young man gotten involved in the gay community. A year previous to this encounter with me on the flight he had gotten saved and he was now serving the Lord. His gay friends just couldn't believe that he could just walk away from this lifestyle but he was following several good teachers on TV and he was attending any Christian conferences he could. Then he said "I believe that God put me next to you on this flight to tell you that your prodigal son is coming home. It may take a long time but he will come home!" I was overwhelmed and couldn't believe how short this flight was when we landed and I had to run to catch my next flight. I may never see this young man again but I watch for him whenever I fly. If I ever get the chance I will thank him and tell him how God used him to help me through a very hard trial.

I have to admit that when he said it could take a long time, possibly five years or more till my son returned, I didn't want to hear it, but he was right. It has taken a long time and he hasn't as of this writing returned, but I know he will. I remember my dad's attitude when my son left, dad knew that my son couldn't outrun God and he refused to worry about it. He was greatly disappointed but he didn't waver.

That precious young man on the flight spoke into my life and I could have missed it if I hadn't taken the time to listen. Those are the types of experiences that make your trial bearable. God is present, He never leaves you but how often do we miss Him because we misjudge a situation or a person who has a word for us. This experience helped me to not so quickly look at the outward appearance and judge a person. Again I am not without fault in this area but I am learning. I catch myself when these wrong thoughts about others come into my mind and take them captive knowing that God can use anyone to speak into my life.

Sometimes we have to be vulnerable. We have to let go of the attitude that builds a wall around us and makes us unable to hear God. There is no trial that we face alone unless we choose to. I have found that most of my trials are too hard and I have no desire to face them alone. The best news is I don't have to go through anything alone and neither do you!

When I think of this young man I am ashamed to admit that he as a new Christian was more eager to be used than I would have let him. How often could God have used me to speak into someone's life but I was afraid of the outcome, afraid I'd be embarrassed or just afraid that God wouldn't be there to help me. We limit God by our unbelief, thinking that we are not good enough or don't know enough. The Bible tells us that we know all things through the Holy Spirit. In our spirits we do know what we need. That is what the Holy Spirit is there for. He leads us when we don't know what to do. He has all the right answers we just need to learn to depend on Him and wait on Him.

1 John 2:20-21 (NKJV) *20But you have an anointing from the Holy One, and you know all things. 21I have not written to you because you do not know the truth, but because you know it, and that no lie is of the truth.*

I think that most Christians who are walking with God want to be used by Him but most of us limit what God can do through us. He is looking for people who will step out in faith and do what this young man on the flight did. I wasn't real receptive at first but he pursued a conversation and I eventually yielded to the push from the Holy Spirit and got involved. In it I was greatly blessed but I could have missed it all!

It makes me wonder what all I have missed out on. Not just in receiving a word but in giving a word. I think this young man was also touched by God on the flight. Our conversation covered a lot and he told me that he was reading through the Bible and I was able to encourage him. He told me about a book he wanted to give to his sister but he couldn't remember the name of it. He said it was written by a lady who is on TV and she talks a lot about the battle in your mind. I knew instantly who he was talking about and I had the book he was talking about. As a matter of fact it was the only book I had that was written by her and I had it in my carry-on bag. I pulled it out and he instantly said "That is the one!" Oh yes God was there and none of the happenings were coincidence. God is in our midst, we just need to allow Him to move and then recognize that He has.

There are many of us who long to be used in a powerful way by God. We want to make a difference and we are just waiting for God to open the doors to something great that we can do. What we have to remember is that God knows when we are ready to be used; He knows what all we need to learn and understand first. This makes me think of Peter. Peter wanted to be great in the Kingdom and he was convinced that he was ready for whatever came and he told the Lord so. Peter thought he was ready for anything.

Matthew 26:33 (NIV) *33Peter replied, "Even if all fall away on account of you, I never will."*

Jesus knew Peter better than Peter knew himself and made a reply that I am sure Peter was convinced couldn't be true.

In verse 34 we read: *34"Truly I tell you," Jesus answered, "this very night, before the rooster crows, you will disown me three times." 35But Peter declared, "Even if I have to die with you, I will never disown you." And all the other disciples said the same.*

This was a trial for Peter and I am sure he learned a lot throughout this time of watching Jesus being crucified, buried and then rising from the dead. What a weekend that must have been! We don't often think about the trial that Peter went through during this time but it was a time of great truth and learning and it changed Peter forever. That is what a trial should do for us, bring change.

So yes trials are not easy, but they are a wonderful learning experience if we allow them to be. We will grow and mature and become who God created us to be. We will fill the shoes that God has for us and fulfill our call just as Peter did. We can enter heaven knowing that we did what we were created to do with our time on earth. Being used by God is the end goal for me. I will go through the trials knowing I will overcome! I will be who God has called me to be and I will live an abundant life!

7

Bite Your Tongue!

· PEOPLE WHO CAN CONTROL THEIR TONGUE
PROVE THEY HAVE PERFECT CONTROL
OVER THEIR LIVES ·

Changing your thinking will change your speech and how you react to various situations. When we see the outcome of the hurtful words we spew and the anger we unleash we often feel shame at our behavior. Some of us will choose to change; others of us will look the other way and try to deny who we have become. For those who bury their heads in the sand, life will go on as usual with disaster happening wherever they go. They leave behind destroyed lives, broken people and wrecked futures, their own included. Then there are those who will see the effects of their words and feel shame and want change. Recognizing the need for change is the first step, the desire to follow through looking for help follows. Change isn't always easy, like I said earlier we are the way we are and have been like that for a very long time. Old habits die hard, but they can be overcome! We are to be over comers, we are destined to win!

1 John 5:4 (NIV) *For everyone born of God overcomes the world. This is the victory that has overcome the world, even our faith.*

Too often we don't see the need to change or we think the struggle to change will be too difficult and we choose to continue on the path we are on. However change is possible and a better life is possible. As a believer in God and what has been done for us we need to change when we see that we have a problem area. The Holy Spirit will point those things out to us and then it is up to us to become the over comer. It starts in our minds and we have to believe that we can overcome and we have to understand that overcoming is what we are called to do! If we do not overcome these situations we will never change our world.

The book of James has some very harsh words to say about the tongue and its effect on the world around us. Let us take a look at anger and what the Word tells us about our anger. First let's recognize that anger is not wrong. Most times when we are angry we end up saying things that we will later regret. It is hard to remember to bite your tongue when anger is present. Anger can easily take over and all common sense leaves the building! It is what we do in anger that makes it wrong. Jesus was angry when he entered the temple and overthrew the tables of those buying and selling. God was angry with the children of Israel and wanted to wipe them out! Our anger is wrong when we sin in our anger and carry it into tomorrow.

Ephesians 4:26–27 (NIV) *26"In your anger do not sin": Do not let the sun go down while you are still angry, and do not give the devil a foothold.*

When we allow anger to fester it builds more anger on the inside of us and then we really cannot think straight. We need to lay our anger aside, forgive and ask for forgiveness when needed, and then move on to better things. Most of us can relate to the fact that we say things in anger that we don't want to say and later regret. Once the words are spoken, no matter how much you want to take them back it is too late. Words kill friendships, destroy families, and cause illness. Your words either bring life or they bring death.

James tells us to not become angry easily because anger will not help us to live the kind of life God wants. (James 1:19-20)

Just before this statement we are told to always be willing to listen and slow to speak. If we follow this advice we are less likely to become angry. Often anger comes when we read into a situation without knowing all the facts. We jump to conclusions and form an opinion without the details. If we are slow to speak and are willing to listen we can save ourselves some frustration.

Learning this truth is something that helps us to change our thinking. We think wrong so we react wrong, let's simplify life and learn to do what the Word tells us to do.

James 1:22-25 (NIV) *22Do not merely listen to the word, and so deceive yourselves. Do what it says. 23Anyone who listens to the word but does not do what it says is like someone who looks at his face in a mirror 24and, after looking at himself, goes away and immediately forgets what he looks like. 25But whoever looks intently into the perfect law that gives freedom, and continues in it—not forgetting what they have heard, but doing it—they will be blessed in what they do.*

So often Christians sit through a service in the church and listen to the Word that is being taught and by midday they have forgotten what the message was even about. We don't take what we have learned and put it to practice in our lives. As long as this is our habit nothing in our lives will improve based on what we heard. It is only when you put to practice what we have heard that it makes an impact on our lives. If we want the blessing it will only come with the doing of what we know to do.

We know our anger is wrong when we hurt those around

us, we know we have said too much when our conscience tells us to be quiet; we know we aren't listening when we should be, and we think we are religious! Well I don't think religion is what God is looking for. He is looking for a follower of His Word, one who will do what he is taught. When we take what we have learned and make it a part of our everyday lives, it impacts those around us and makes a difference in the world. That is Christianity not religion.

One of my favorite little children's songs is "This little Light of Mine" let it shine, let it shine, let it shine! A hidden light makes no impact on those around it, the light on the table shines for all to see. The same is true of our lives. If we are darkness in a dark world our lives will not change anything for the better. Uncontrolled anger is darkness and no light is in it. A light in a dark world shines brightly for all to see. When you feel yourself becoming angry you can stop yourself from saying hateful words and you can become light to a situation. It is hard to be light in anger. If you keep your cool you can be the one that brings light to the situation. When your light is shining people notice that something about you is different, often they will want what you have. People are attracted to light and people will be attracted to you when your light shines.

Matthew 5:16 *16In the same way, let your light shine before others, that they may see your good deeds and glorify your Father in heaven.*

A Christian in hiding makes no impact on those around him but one who shines his light will change the world! By renewing our minds, transforming our thinking we change everything and it affects everyone who we come in contact with.

Our tongue can very quickly tell the world who we really are. There is so much in the Bible about our tongues, it is very sobering. Every one of us deals with this problem. Some people talk too much, some people are known for their negative attitude and talk, it is known because of the words that come out of their mouths. Other people are known as short tempered; some are rude, while others are gossips. The world is full of people who have a talking problem! Then we go to church and are all spiritual playing the opposite roll and trying to portray the holiness we aren't!

On the other hand we all know people who are controlled in speech. They are careful and you can tell they are thinking before they talk. We see these people as wise people and they seldom make a fool of themselves in anger. I know a lady who is so slow in speech that sometimes when I am taking to her I think she didn't hear me. She is never in a hurry with words. You can tell that she is carefully considering what she is going to say. That is hard on people like me but I realize that I need people like this in my life. It reminds me that I need to slow down a bit and take more time to think about what I am going to say. It also teaches me patience!

In anger we speak harsh words and say things we regret, and then we go to church to worship an all knowing God who probably looks at us and thinks we need to get it together! James tells us that the two do not go together.

James compares it to a spring that cannot bring forth both fresh water and salt water. Only our mouths are capable of delivering two very different things. He also compares it to a tree that is known by its fruit, an apple tree is not going to produce grapes! We think we are fooling people but are never fooling God. God knows everything that is going on in our lives and we are never able to hide it from Him. We can try to fool people but our lives give us away. Our actions and our words tell the world who we really are.

You cannot live like this and then expect the abundant life that is talked about in scripture. A new way of thinking helps us to see the truth of our ways and when the truth comes we are set free. The truth about our tongue is that it cannot be tamed! That is just a simple but painful truth. How then are we ever going to change this about ourselves?

James 3:7-12 (NIV) *7All kinds of animals, birds, reptiles and sea creatures are being tamed and have been tamed by mankind, 8but no human being can tame the tongue. It is a restless evil, full of deadly poison.*

9With the tongue we praise our Lord and Father, and with it we curse human beings, who have been made in God's likeness. 10Out of the same mouth come praise and cursing. My brothers and sisters, this should not be. 11Can both fresh water and salt water flow from the same spring? 12My brothers and sisters, can a fig tree bear olives, or a grapevine bear figs? Neither can a salt spring produce fresh water.

We can see that animals can be tamed, even reptiles can be tamed but the tongue cannot be tamed. Without the Holy Spirit in our lives there are many things that we cannot do. We need the Holy Spirit to help us to be the kind of people that God wants us to be.

This scripture tells us that the tongue is a deadly poison. If you have ever been around an angry parent and heard the words that are shouted at their children you know what poison words look like. Those words can break a child and they will have an affect all his or her life. The poison from a parent can destroy the child's life. Only God can restore the child's life and He can use people to speak good into the child's life. You can be used by God to save the life of a child.

I own a number of retail shops and I am always amazed at

how many parents come in to a store and yell at their children. You can tell by the child's attitude toward the parent that being yelled at, being threatened and belittled is normal for them. Recently at Wal Mart I saw something similar. A young girl about eight years old wanted something and her mother was shouting at her and hitting her on the head telling her to be quiet. The young girl was throwing a temper tantrum screaming and crying then throwing herself on the floor. Neither the mother nor the daughter seemed to have any idea that they were in public. A bit later as I was paying I heard the girl still crying loudly somewhere at the back of the store and before I left they were at the front of the store and the girl was sitting in the shopping cart still crying. I took the opportunity to explain to the young cashier that when you don't discipline your children at home they will not obey you in public. These types of situations seem to be becoming more prevalent as parents are not raising children Gods way. It doesn't make any difference how much yelling the parent does the child does what he wants to, they know the threats are empty words. They already know that there will be no punishment for not listening. Second, to him yelling is normal. I feel sorry for these children because I see that they are not being taught at home and if the child is not taught at home you cannot teach him in public.

Unfortunately children raised in this environment will either never understand the value of words or have to learn once they enter the outside world and that can be very difficult and painful for them. The world doesn't show mercy and is quick to condemn. The bad habit that was born at home goes with the child through adulthood and they may have a hard time learning to change that behavior as an adult. Only when they meet the Savior can real change come.

Our language and tone of voice says volumes about us. Taming the tongue is a day to day every day practice and without the help of the Holy Spirit it is pretty much impossible. We need change!

Proverbs 15:4 (NIV) *⁴The soothing tongue is a tree of life, but a perverse tongue crushes the spirit*

When a Christian is filled with the Holy Spirit change comes, but our minds still have to be renewed with the right things. The more we study the Word of God the more right food we give our minds the more we will change and renew our minds.

A number of years ago my husband and I traveled through the state of Washington. We took time to take a helicopter ride over Mt. St. Helens and we saw the destruction of the volcano. The burned forests, the trees thrown over by the force of the volcano and the black ash are all that was left behind. It was a total destruction of the mountain and a good portion of the mountain was missing from the top.

This is what our words can do to our children, our co-workers, our employees. Our words are destructive when we do not harness our mouths. Our mouth becomes a volcano. We never stop to think about the damage we have done. Often we are not there later to see the affect our words had on a person. A life is a fragile thing and it can be very easily destroyed by our careless words.

Fresh water from rains can restore a burned forest and green life will eventually return but it takes many years for that forest to return to the original state it was in before the fire. Fresh water is like healing words to a wounded person. Life to the wounded can be restored but just like the forest it can take a long time.

We desperately need a new way of thinking. We need to stop, think and sometimes cool off before we spout words we shouldn't say. Learn to pray quietly under your breath and ask the Holy Spirit to help you stay calm and to have the right words to say so that you do not destroy the other person. I often use this practice even during a conversation. At times while the other person is talking I am asking the Holy Spirit to help me say the right things and not to even put into words the things I shouldn't say. God protect me from my tongue!

In Proverbs we find some good advice about biting our tongues, Proverbs 13:3 (NIV) *³Those who guard their lips preserve their lives, but those who speak rashly will come to ruin*

Remember that God loves the other person as much as He loves you and He wants to protect that person from words you are about to say.

Proverbs 18:21 (NCV) *²¹What you say can mean life or death. Those who speak with care will be rewarded.*

Your words will either bring life or they will bring death, which one do you want to be known for? Think about a person who has said words to you that built you up and what it did for you. You have the power to do the same for someone else. On the other hand most of us can easily recall unkind words that were spoken to us at some time and recall the pain it caused. Carelessly spoken words are costly and can do great damage, or well thought out words can build a person up. Either way there is a harvest based on the words that were spoken.

Proverbs 12:18 (NIV) *¹⁸The words of the reckless pierce like swords, but the tongue of the wise brings healing.*

If you grew up in a home where you were belittled and had low self esteem you can do better for your children and your grandchildren. You can change the cycle and speak words that will bring life to those around you. Stop the flow of profanity coming out of your mouth. Renew your thinking to be God like. Be a part of the abundant life and share good things with those around you. Do unto others as you would have them do unto you (there it is again).

Another tidbit I found in James is this comment;

James 3:2 (NIV) *²We all stumble in many ways. Anyone who is never at fault in what they say is perfect, able to keep their whole body in check*

What a thought! If you are never at fault in what you say you are perfect and you are able to keep your whole body in check! Since we know we are not perfect we can know that this is not something we have achieved. However knowing that if we work on perfecting our words and the things we say then we are also working on perfecting our lives. Learning to control our words sounds like a good way to lose some weight, after all your whole body being perfect would include that, wouldn't it? That is worth giving some thought to!

In Ephesians we have such a beautiful reminder from Paul about how our talk should be.

Ephesians 4:29-32 (NIV) *²⁹Do not let any unwholesome talk come out of your mouths, but only what is helpful for building others up according to their needs, that it may benefit those who listen. ³⁰And do not grieve the Holy Spirit of God, with whom you were sealed for the day of redemption. ³¹Get rid of all bitterness, rage and anger, brawling and slander, along with every form of malice. ³²Be kind and compassionate to one another, forgiving each other, just as in Christ God forgave you.*

I believe that pretty well sums it up in one nice package. This is who we should strive to become. For many people this is completely contrary to how life has been lived. We tend to be selfish, thinking only of ourselves but this shows us what kind of people we should be.

Throughout the Bible there are more scriptures on our speech, how we communicate, and the things we say than any other topic. God must be serious about this and there must be great value in learning this lesson. So we will look just a bit further and see what Solomon has to say about this topic in the book of Proverbs.

In Proverbs 3:20-24 (NIV) we see these words of wisdom from him.

[20]My son, pay attention to what I say; turn your ear to my words.

[21]Do not let them out of your sight, keep them within your heart;

[22]for they are life to those who find them and health to one's whole body.

[23]Above all else, guard your heart, for everything you do flows from it.

[24]Keep your mouth free of perversity; keep corrupt talk far from your lips.

Here we are told to pay attention to the words of wisdom and not let them depart from us. We all want a good life and this is a good place to start. Or how about this from Solomon:

Proverbs 6:16-19 (NIV)

[16]There are six things the Lord hates,

seven that are detestable to him:

[17]haughty eyes,

a lying tongue,

hands that shed innocent blood,

[18]a heart that devises wicked schemes,

feet that are quick to rush into evil,

[19]a false witness who pours out lies

and a person who stirs up conflict in the community.

Notice that out of the seven things listed that the Lord hates, three of them have to do with the mouth, a lying tongue, a false witness and a person who stirs up conflict. How often have we been in the middle of some of these things?

The words we speak have power. With words God spoke the universe into existence and with words we speak many things into existence in our own lives. We speak our futures into existence; whether for the good or for bad. There is power in the tongue. For the sake of those around us and for our own sakes it would do us good to learn this incredibly powerful lesson. It can change our lives! Decide now that you want these things to be a part of your life, renew your mind to the truth of this message and put into practice what you have learned.

James 1:22 (NIV) *22Do not merely listen to the word, and so deceive yourselves. Do what it says.*

Let us also remember that what is inside of us will come out whether it is good or bad. There are people who try to conceal what is inside but under pressure the truth falls from their lips. Make sure that you are filling up on good so that good will come out when you speak.

Luke 6:45 (NIV) *45A good man brings good things out of the good stored up in his heart, and an evil man brings evil things out of the evil stored up in his heart. For the mouth speaks what the heart is full of.*

8

Thinking Highly of Yourself

· HAVE NO CONFIDENCE IN THE FLESH ·

Romans 12:3 (NIV) *³For by the grace given me I say to every one of you: Do not think of yourself more highly than you ought, but rather think of yourself with sober judgment, in accordance with the faith God has distributed to each of you*

Now this is truly a thought that goes against our values today. We live in a society where everything is about me, what makes me happy, what fulfills my life, what do I want to do or where do I want to go? People are so consumed with thoughts of their own happiness that few people show any concern for others in their world. They think quite highly of themselves but not of anyone else.

A great example of this is the fact that today there are many children growing up without fathers. Their fathers are missing for one reason or another and are often just consumed with their own desires and they have no time for the children they have fathered. They are selfish and greedy and will not humble themselves or be responsible to go home and raise their children putting them ahead of their own desires. Therefore thousands of children are growing up without a father figure in the home. How are these young sons going to learn to be responsible fathers in the future without an example to learn from? Unfortunately there is a great chance that they will grow up to be as irresponsible as their fathers were and the cycle continues. It has been one of the downfalls of our great nation. The mothers that are left to raise the children are often employed trying to make ends meet and are not home to care for the children. When they get home from a long day at work the last thing they often want to do is spend any quality time with their children, they are exhausted from trying to be both a mother and a father. Many people are doing the best they know how to do but the fact that our country is going in the wrong direction at break neck speed shows us that it is not working.

Parents need to parent their children and raise them thinking of them ahead of their own needs. We have no business bringing children into the world then being too selfish to take care of their needs first. The same is true of marriage. When you get married you need to take care of your spouse, you cannot have a good marriage if you do not learn to give to each other. Your marriage has to be a priority and when children are added to the union you really will often not have much time for yourself. You have to think of the others in your life to have a successful family life.

There are also thousands of people who think too highly of themselves comparing themselves to others and looking down their noses at those they esteem to be in a lower class than they are. God didn't create people in different classes, people have done that to others forgetting that God created all of us and when we get to heaven we will not be divided into groups of "haves" and "have nots".

We are clearly taught in scripture that this is not pleasing to God. God has given each of us our own lives and He has individual plans for each of us. It takes all of us doing our part and caring for each other to accomplish all He has for us. If you do not do the part God created you for He will find someone else to do it and they will get your blessing.

Romans 12:4-8 (NIV) *⁴For just as each of us has one body with many members, and these members do not all have the same function, ⁵so in Christ we, though many, form one body, and each member belongs to all the others. ⁶We have different gifts, according to the grace given to each of us. If your gift is prophesying, then prophesy in accordance with your faith; ⁷if it is serving, then serve; if it is teaching, then teach; ⁸if it is to encourage, then give encouragement; if it is giving, then give generously; if it is to lead, do it diligently; if it is to show mercy, do it cheerfully.*

Part of renewing our minds is to start recognizing that we all have a role to play and a life to live for God. Not one of us is more important to God than anyone else. God created the person you look down on just as He created you. We have to learn not to judge others and think so highly of ourselves. We have to learn to follow the leading of the Holy Spirit and do what we are told to do. This means we have to get past the fear that we could have heard wrong, isn't it worth taking the chance that you heard from God and possibly saving someone from an eternity without God?

It truly takes a community to raise a child in today's world! If you don't have any loved ones who are not walking with the Lord then believe me you have no idea how much a mother prays that a Christian out there somewhere will be there for their adult child and do what God is placing in their hearts to do. I believe it is a prayer that every parent of unsaved family members prays for and you could be that person! God has something for each of us to do and when we feel that tug in our hearts it is often God giving us a gentle nudge to step out in faith to fill a need.

James 2:2-7 (NIV) *²Suppose a man comes into your meeting wearing a gold ring and fine clothes, and a poor man in filthy old clothes also comes in. ³If you show special attention to the man wearing fine clothes and say, "Here's a good seat for you," but say to the poor man, "You stand there" or "Sit on the floor by my feet," ⁴have you not discriminated among yourselves and become judges with evil thoughts?*

⁵Listen, my dear brothers and sisters: Has not God chosen those who are poor in the eyes of the world to be rich in faith and to inherit the kingdom He promised those who love Him? ⁶But you have dishonored the poor. Is it not the rich who are exploiting you? Are they not the ones who are dragging you into court? ⁷Are they not the ones who are blaspheming the noble name of Him to whom you belong?

How often are we guilty of judging someone by the clothes they wear, the car they drive or other foolish things like the way they walk? (Well let's face it, it is all foolish) I have been guilty of this, as a matter of fact when I think to earlier today I remember making a comment about someone I used to think was nice but his fame has gone to his head and now he struts! I said "he is cocky and arrogant!" Maybe he is and maybe I just see him differently but it is not up to me to be his judge. I have no right imposing my opinion of him on others and swaying how they look at him unless I say something to build him up, not tear him down! I do not know this person, I have gone against God and

I need to quit that and change my thinking. God does not love me more than He loves this man. If I sense a problem I need to ask God to help him and to help me to change my attitude.

James further reminds us of the royal law found in scripture, "Love your neighbor as yourself" He clearly tells us that if we do this we are doing right but if we do not then we are sinning, then we are guilty of breaking Gods law. He even goes further and tells us that if we break this one law we are guilty of breaking all the laws!

James 2:10-13 (NIV) *10For whoever keeps the whole law and yet stumbles at just one point is guilty of breaking all of it. 11For he who said, "You shall not commit adultery," also said, "You shall not murder." If you do not commit adultery but do commit murder, you have become a lawbreaker.*

12Speak and act as those who are going to be judged by the law that gives freedom, 13because judgment without mercy will be shown to anyone who has not been merciful. Mercy triumphs over judgment.

Oh how we don't want to know this. We want to believe that we are not guilty but we are. Without Jesus and what He did for us there is no hope for any of us. We are all guilty and we all need a savior, (That includes that person you don't really care for). Thank you Jesus, our Savior!

In Matthew 23 Jesus is talking about the Teachers of the Law and the Pharisees and how they like to take the best seat in the house and be recognized as the most important people.

Matthew 23:5-7 *5"Everything they do is done for people to see: They make their phylacteries wide and the tassels on their garments long; 6they love the place of honor at banquets and the most important seats in the synagogues; 7they love to be greeted with respect in the marketplaces and to be called 'Rabbi' by others.*

These people looked down their long noses on everyone who was not one of them and thought more highly of themselves than they should have. A few verses later Jesus reminds them that we are to be servants to all.

Matthew 23:11-12 (NIV) *11 The greatest among you will be your servant. 12 For those who exalt themselves will be humbled, and those who humble themselves will be exalted.*

We need to humble ourselves, become a servant to all and allow God or other people to give us honor rather than trying to honor ourselves. We want the world to see how great we are and all that we have accomplished. We brag about ourselves and then post it all on social media to make sure the world knows how great we are. Social media has some benefits but this issue of making sure that everyone you know, knows about all your great accomplishments is self promotion and pride. It stinks and I don't think God is pleased with some of the things that people are posting. When we honor ourselves God won't and we need to realize that honor and promotion that comes from God is far superior to any self promotion we can ever do. We need to allow others to honor us.

Luke 14:8-11 (NIV) *8 "When someone invites you to a wedding feast, do not take the place of honor, for a person more distinguished than you may have been invited. 9 If so, the host who invited both of you will come and say to you, 'Give this person your seat.' Then, humiliated, you will have to take the least important place. 10 But when you are invited, take the lowest place, so that when your host comes, he will say to you, 'Friend, move up to a better place.' Then you will be honored in the presence of all the other guests. 11 For all those who exalt themselves will be humbled, and those who humble themselves will be exalted."*

Notice that when you exalt yourself you will be humbled.

Again this goes against what we tend to believe. We live in fear that no one will notice how great we are or what great things we have accomplished. We seem to think that we can promote ourselves better than waiting on God to promote us at the right time. When you really look at this you can see just how foolish this is on our part. Is God not much more capable of honoring us than we are? Does He not know when we are ready to be honored? Do we truly believe we know more about ourselves and know what is best for us better than God does?

We need to let God be God and keep ourselves from thinking we know what is best. We need to quit thinking so highly of ourselves that we have to let the world know about "me". In due season, when the time is right God who knows exactly when we are ready for promotion will take care of promoting us. There are times we think we are ready for promotion or honor but God knows it will go to our heads and we will become proud. There are things we have to learn first, then once we have learned and we have more understanding, when the time is right God will do a much better job at honoring us than we can ever do on our own.

This reminds me again of Peter who was so sure of himself and he insisted that he knew more than Jesus did. Peter was not as ready as he thought he was. In time, after some hard lessons Peter was ready and he was used mightily by God. I also think of Saul who was so proud and arrogant until he was knocked off his horse and met the Savior. He was used by God and his writings are now all over the world. We learn much from his letters to the churches but until he was brought down a bit he was far from ready for what God had planned for him.

We need to quit thinking so highly of ourselves and instead look around us and recognize the wonderful things others are doing. We need to honor others and be humble about our own achievements allowing God to honor us at the right time.

We live in a world full of prideful and arrogant people. Self promoters who are starving for attention will do anything to be noticed. There are people everywhere who pick their friends by choosing to spend time with those who they feel will see how great they are. Other times we look around us and try to make connections with people who are popular or have money thinking there might be something in it for ourselves. We seem to be starved for recognition. We have accomplished something great and no one takes notice and we are offended and hurt.

As followers of Jesus we need to be different, we need to allow God to be the one that promotes us but it takes a lot of waiting, and waiting and waiting! There are many people who are waiting on God and learning patience while they wait. Patience is a big part of the lives of Christians. One way or another we will learn to be patient. There are times when it sure feels like God is in no hurry and we want to help him along, but we need to keep our hands off and let God take the reins.

Earlier in this book I touched on pride and pride is often what keeps us from having patience. We are so afraid that our time in the spotlight will pass us by and we have to promote ourselves before we go unnoticed. In our rush and panic we promote before our time and we can miss the whole plan of God for our lives. God can work around the mess we have made of things but now it takes more time than it would have had we just had some patience! We have to learn this; it truly is a new way of thinking!

We need to remember what the Bible has to say about pride. If you need help in this I recommend that you go to biblegateway.com and enter "pride" or "proud" and just see all the scriptures about this subject! Here are just a few.

Proverbs 29:23 (NIV) *23Pride brings a person low, but the lowly in spirit gain honor*

James 4:6 (NIV) *6But he gives us more grace. That is why Scripture says: "God opposes the proud but shows favor to the humble."*

Proverbs 3:34 (NIV) *34He mocks proud mockers but shows favor to the humble and oppressed.*

Proverbs 16:5 (NIV) *5The Lord detests all the proud of heart. Be sure of this: They will not go unpunished.*

1 John 2:16 (NIV) *16For everything in the world—the lust of the flesh, the lust of the eyes, and the pride of life—comes not from the Father but from the world.*

Our pride causes us to think too highly of ourselves and we have to remember that being prideful will lead to disaster.

Proverbs 16:18 (NIV) *18Pride goes before destruction, a haughty spirit before a fall.*

I have recently heard a teaching on pride and humility. They are opposites however we often do not understand what true humility is. We think that a humble person is one who denies himself, is always in the shadows, never allowing himself to receive any credit for any accomplishments. That is not humility and it is certainly not the life of one who overcomes. God blessed each of us with gifts and talents. When we deny that we have been given these gifts we are not showing appreciation to our Father who gave these gifts to us. When we do something well and are recognized for it there is nothing wrong in saying thank you. The key is in giving God the credit, you are the vessel that God used. God should receive the glory that is due Him. I think we all want to be used by God but do we then show our appreciation by giving God the credit, are our motives pure, and do we have the right attitude? These are all things we need to look at as possible reasons that we are not being used by God as we would like to be.

Jesus said of himself:

Matthew 11:29 (NIV) *²⁹Take my yoke upon you and learn from me, for I am gentle and humble in heart, and you will find rest for your souls.*

Jesus himself said he is humble, yet he drove people out of the temple with a whip! In our natural minds we would say that anyone who says he is humble is a proud and arrogant person and we would think that a humble person would never drive people out of a building with a whip. Humbleness according to Webster's means: a modest or low view of one's own importance. Jesus wasn't saying He wasn't worthy of praise or important but He came as a servant of all, He came in humility to serve.

Luke 22:27 (NIV) *²⁷For who is greater, the one who is at the table or the one who serves? Is it not the one who is at the table? But I am among you as one who serves.*

We all want to be served, we are proud and want recognition and yet Jesus told us to be one who serves, like He was. How often do we serve? How do we serve? Do we think we are less when we do serve? These are all questions we need to ask ourselves.

When we are the ones being served we need to show our appreciation and not be haughty and demanding. Remember the one doing the serving is the one who is being Christ like. We need to recognize the servant who is serving us and be gracious. When we are the one serving others we need to serve with the attitude that it is an honor to be serving.

Instead of looking how and where we can be in order to be served we need to see where we can go to be of service to others. The little things we do for others will be appreciated.

God will give each of us opportunity to be of service and to do something nice for someone else. Many of us want to do nice things for others but we tend to be so busy that we miss opportunities to bless others even in small things.

Inside we all know that the feeling you get from doing for others is far superior to the feeling you get from being served. It is not that being served isn't a good feeling but being the servant is a better feeling. There is satisfaction in being the servant, it fulfills us and we want to do even more the next time.

We need to learn to trust, wait, humble ourselves, and wait some more. In due time it will be our turn and when the time is right there is no feeling that will compare and God has plans for each of us that are far superior to anything we can even imagine. We limit ourselves because we don't see what God sees. Let God be the one who decides when and how to promote you. In the meantime do not think of yourself more highly than you ought, instead humble yourself and in due time your promotion will come.

9

Waiting, Waiting, Waiting...

· THEY THAT WAIT UPON THE LORD ·

I love the parable of the sower found in Matthew.

Matthew 13:3-9 (NIV) *3"A farmer went out to sow his seed. 4As he was scattering the seed, some fell along the path, and the birds came and ate it up. 5Some fell on rocky places, where it did not have much soil. It sprang up quickly, because the soil was shallow. 6But when the sun came up, the plants were scorched, and they withered because they had no root. 7Other seed fell among thorns, which grew up and choked the plants. 8Still other seed fell on good soil, where it produced a crop—a hundred, sixty or thirty times what was sown. 9Whoever has ears, let them hear."*

Then in James chapter 5 (vs. 7-8) we read the following information also about the seed.

7Therefore be patient, brethren, until the coming of the Lord. See how the farmer waits for the precious fruit of the earth, waiting patiently for it until it receives the early and latter rain. 8You also be patient. Establish your hearts, for the coming of the Lord is at hand.

Farmers know they have to plant then wait, they wait a long time for the harvest and in the meantime they take care of the seed that they have planted. They spend time weeding, watering and feeding the seed. They do not get impatient and dig the seed up to see if it is still there. They know they have planted and they know that there is waiting involved.

Sometimes we can have a word from God but time goes by and we don't see anything happening. This is a good time to remember that Gods word is the seed, He has promised a harvest and we need to believe that God does what He says He will do.

We cannot become impatient and start declaring negative things about what we feel should be happening. Believe me when the time is right the harvest, the promise will come. God knows more about good timing than we do. We think everything should be now but that is not how God works.

As I wait for an answer to a long time problem I have periodically had confirmation that God has not forgotten me. When the trial first began I needed a lot from God, I felt lost and hopeless but as time went on I learned to let God take the problem that I cannot solve anyways and just relax. If I had my way the answer would have come years ago, but at the same time I want the right results to the problem. I do not want a temporary fix I want an absolute fix. That means I have to allow it to be on Gods timetable not mine.

Not so long ago I asked God if he had forgotten me. In my spirit I knew he hadn't forgotten but because I have a relationship with my Father I was able to talk to Him about how I felt and He gave me a very clear confirmation that He has not forgotten me. That is what a relationship with God is, two way communication. I still have to wait.

We have also all heard that the Word of God is alive and active.

Hebrews 4:12 (NIV) *12For the word of God is alive and active. Sharper than any double-edged sword, it penetrates even to dividing soul and spirit, joints and marrow; it judges the thoughts and attitudes of the heart.*

Since the Word of God is a seed and a seed is alive I know that Gods word is alive just as scripture tells me. Now it is up to me to use the Word of God and confess it with my mouth. I can confess my belief that God's word is true or I can complain about how long it is taking. One confession will bring faith to my spirit the other will bring defeat. The words I speak always have results.

Seed, time and harvest consist of a lot of time and lots waiting! Most generally a long time, just like it takes time for seed that is planted in the ground to come forth and we have to wait, we need to take the seed of God and allow it to grow and teach us all things.

We on the other hand want everything in an instant and so we have to train ourselves to think and behave differently. We can see the truth in farming and the time it takes to produce a crop but we need to learn to apply that to our lives. We have to learn to wait on Gods timing for things. We need to spend time meditating on the scripture allowing it to take root and when it takes root it will change us from the inside. We have to read, understand what we are reading, and then meditate on it till we see it become alive in our lives. If you do not understand what a scripture is saying then find a different translation or someone who understands scripture and find out what it means so that you have understanding. It does you no good to think you understand what is being said then spend time trying to learn something that is incorrect. With today's technology you can see as many translations as you need without buying ten different translations. This is making good use of modern technology.

God wants us to understand His Word and He wants us to learn. Understanding truth is what sets us free. The wrong truth is not truth! Meditate on truth.

When we apply patience, humility and servant hood to our lives and learn to see in others what Jesus sees we can make a difference. In today's world these three things have become less and less popular. It goes against everything in our society, but then we are not here to be like the world we are here to be different. We are called to be salt and light and in our current world it is not hard to be either but it does take courage to stand for what we know is the truth. Let's humble ourselves and become servants to those around us, let us be patient and show patience to others. Let's bring others into the family by showing them what Christianity really is. We are only effective if we are being salt or light and salt that loses its flavor is worthless! Let's not lose our flavor, let's let our lights shine and let's make a difference in a dark world.

We are living in the times that were talked about in 2 Timothy.

2 Timothy 3 (NIV) *¹But mark this: There will be terrible times in the last days. ²People will be lovers of themselves, lovers of money, boastful, proud, abusive, disobedient to their parents, ungrateful, unholy, ³without love, unforgiving, slanderous, without self-control, brutal, not lovers of the good, ⁴treacherous, rash, conceited, lovers of pleasure rather than lovers of God— ⁵having a form of godliness but denying its power. Have nothing to do with such people.*

Patience has a way of calming our spirits. When we are calm we are less likely to be like the people described above. A patient person understands that things take time. Patience on its own will not keep you from becoming like these people but a patient person with control of their tongue and a relationship with the Father will be different. They will be a light to people who are out of control in these ways.

If we see ourselves in any of the description above then we need to reevaluate a few things. God says we should have nothing to do with people like this. These are the people who think they know more than God. They are not patiently waiting for God, they are not serving others, and they are definitely not humble. They are completely consumed with self. Can you see the lack of patience in the descriptions of the people described in these verses? There is nothing here that resembles patience, humility or servant hood.

If you have ever been at a restaurant and seen someone mistreat a server who is trying to please, you have seen how ugly it is. Servers are often busy trying to please a number of people. Many of us go out to eat once or twice a week and we know we may have to wait for a table, we know the restaurant is busy and yet we go in with an attitude that we need good service and we need it quickly. We should know better than that but it doesn't stop us from being impatient and often rude when things don't go the way we think they should.

Patience is a virtue, one we desperately need. We need to get over ourselves and our own image of how important we are and become patient servants.

I have heard from the youth in our church about the experiences they have when they go to a poor country or even a poverty stricken community in the United States. Often in these areas people have very little in the way of the luxury we live with on a day to day basis. Mission trips are a great place to learn about the value of serving. It is often here that you can also learn patience. In third world countries they have so little and they often are found waiting, waiting for help to arrive, waiting and often with very little hope.

We live in a world far removed from the mission field, not that we are not a mission field ourselves but our surroundings are a completely different world. We are impatient and we want what we want and we want it now!

The times we are living in are changing rapidly and the world seems to move faster and faster with each year. All around us we see moral decline. We see more and more perverse things happening. When we apply the truths of humility, patience and servant hood we stand out in the crowd. We are different. We have every opportunity to shine in a dark world but it also takes resolve to be that person. We have to learn to stop and think before reacting. If we would do that more we would have more light to shine. Instead we jump in with both feet and make a mess out of things and then it is too late and we have lost an opportunity to be a light in a dark situation.

Patience speaks volumes; the world around us is not patient. When you have to wait in a line with others you can look around and see the frustration on faces, people do not like to wait. There are many times when we know we are going to have to wait, we need to think ahead and determine beforehand that we will wait and we will wait patiently.

On several occasions I have had flights cancelled and have had to stand in line waiting to be rescheduled for a flight. It is amazing how mad people get about these things. The anger they have is not going to do any favors for them. One time when we were traveling in Hawaii we decided to rent a car for the day. When we got to the rental place there were number of people ahead of us most of them demanding this or that. They mistreated the poor employees who were trying to please everyone. My husband and I waited patiently in line and when it was our turn we smiled and were happy. The employee looked at us with a smile and thanked us for being nice. Then she gave us a convertible for the day at the same cost of the cheaper car we had booked. That is favor and all we did was be a light in dark surroundings. We were patient and kind and God blessed us with a much nicer car. We had so much fun with that car and we drove all over the island enjoying the fresh breeze and sunshine.

It takes patience when you are waiting for others and it takes patience when you are waiting for answers to problems from God. Learning to communicate with the Holy Spirit who lives inside of you will help you be patient as well. Trusting that God's timing is always better than yours will help you be patient.

Patience is a value that we all need to develop in our lives. Your family will notice, your friends will notice and you will be seen as a wise person, one who has the right values.

There is often ridicule and criticism associated with people who have values. What used to be right is now wrong and what was wrong is now right! How did we get so far from the truth? The world seems to get more and more critical of Christians and they don't hesitate to let us know what they think of us, could it be because too many of us have not lived the life of an over comer? How has our attitude, our lack of patience, our short temper and lack of love for the non believers played into the current state of things as they are today?

Recently I made a purchase at a local store where I have shopped before. I have always written out company checks when I shop at this store and have never had anyone ask me for an ID, but this time when I went to pay the sales clerk asked for my ID and I did not respond well. Actually I made a fool of myself! I did not treat her like I would want to be treated. I was not Christ like in any way or fashion. My language was clean but my behavior spoke louder than any words I could have said. Now I am sure that she was only doing her job and she had no idea who I was although I own a business less than a mile down the road. It does not matter, I was wrong, I know I was wrong and when I was acting the way I was acting I knew I was wrong but I did it anyway, now isn't that just the dumbest thing I could have done? Instantly I developed a reputation with that girl and she most likely has now determined in her mind what kind of person I am, she has judged me based on my behavior at the time. She will now remember me the next time I come in and she will probably try to keep her distance. There was nothing I did right in this situation. It will now be harder for me to redeem myself with her when I could have just been polite and gone to my car to get my ID. I could have been completely different and could have left that store feeling good about myself, but no I chose otherwise. Like I said, I have learned but I have not overcome. I still have a ways to go! I did not treat her the way I would want to be treated or how I would want others to treat my employees. I most likely have been judged as an unreasonable person and I did it to myself!

Now I get to put another principle into play, that of humility, but that is another story. The next time I go into this store I will go in thinking differently and I will apologize to this poor clerk for my bad behavior. I made a fool of myself and now I have to work even harder to redeem myself. It's called redemption; it's what the Father did for me! In the meantime I have not been a good example of Christianity.

Some Christians think that pointing out every one's fault

or at least what they see as a fault will make a sinner want to be a Christian, it isn't working! Love is what wins people over. We want to win the world for Jesus but often go about it the wrong way.

We need to have our hearts and our minds set on Jesus and know where our help comes from or we will crumble under the scrutiny of the world. We have to keep our minds in line with the Word of God and remember that God is in charge no matter how it looks. All men will bow to the name of Jesus before this is over. It is our responsibility to represent Christ to a lost world. By renewing our minds and living the way Jesus taught us to we will shine and the light we shine will make a difference. Every soul saved is one that Satan doesn't get, each one of them counts!

10

Giving

· GIVE AND IT WILL BE GIVEN TO YOU,
GOOD MEASURE, PRESSED DOWN,
SHAKEN TOGETHER AND RUNNING OVER ·

He who has the most toys wins! Wrong! He who has the most toys has a lot of stuff that someone else is going to have to deal with when he dies! Stuff is just stuff! Let's get over having to own everything. Who would ever have believed that we would rent storage units to store all of the stuff we have accumulated, stuff we don't need and don't use. What a shame!

My father passed away five years ago and after his death we learned how true the above statements are. Things are just things and you are not taking any of it with you when you die, worse yet there are not too many people who really care about all the things you have accumulated. Dad was not a man with lots of stuff but what he did have we still had to deal with. You can read about my fathers life in my book "Challenges Choices and Changes." John Schrock was a great man and I am proud to be his daughter. My dad was a happy man and he didn't have to have "things" to make him happy.

When he passed to his new home I started to see "things" in a different light. I started packing up things I own and taking them to our church thrift store. We are all guilty of having things we haven't used in years but for some reason we hang on to it thinking that maybe someday I will need it. The truth is that if you will just pack it up and donate it to someone who will use it you will save your family from having to deal with it once you are gone.

If all of us did this the thrift stores and donation centers would never have a shortage of supplies for those in need, and we would never miss the things we donate! That is a great idea, and you know it so why not do it? You will find that once you start it is hard to stop and you will enjoy living around less clutter. You will also feel good about helping others with things you don't need any ways. Someone out there will appreciate your donation.

Giving to others goes against our selfish interests because somehow we really do believe that the one with the most toys wins. We have our values messed up and it is complicating our lives. Let's simplify our own lives and help others by giving not only our extras but giving our best.

Genesis 12:2 (NIV) *²"I will make you into a great nation, and I will bless you; I will make your name great, and you will be a blessing.*

God blesses us so that we can be a blessing to others. So many times we tend to think that if I only had more money I would be able to help others. We tell ourselves that as soon as we have our bills paid off we will help others, it is always later. God wants to bless us but we have to first see that everything we have isn't ours, it is His. He has blessed us and we have horded instead of helping others.

Genesis 13:8-9 (NIV) *⁸So Abram said to Lot, "Let's not have any quarreling between you and me, or between your herders and mine, for we are close relatives. ⁹Is not the whole land before you? Let's part company. If you go to the left, I'll go to the right; if you go to the right, I'll go to the left."*

Abraham gave Lot a choice and Lot chose what looked best. Abraham went in the other direction and was blessed everywhere he went. He was willing to give and ended up getting more than he gave. In the end Lot had nothing. Everything was lost while Abraham continued to walk with the Lord and trust that God would take care of him just as He had told him He would.

You cannot out give God. There are so many things that we can give and so many areas in life where giving gives us freedom and peace. Let's take some time to look at some of these things that Jesus talks about.

· GIVE A BLESSING ·

1 Peter 3:9 (NIV) *⁹Do not repay evil with evil or insult with insult. On the contrary, repay evil with blessing, because to this you were called so that you may inherit a blessing*

This just doesn't sound like the way we live. It doesn't make sense to the natural mind that we should bless someone who has treated us in an evil way or that we shouldn't hurl an insult back at the person who has insulted us.

I challenge you to do exactly what this verse says. Just try it and see what it does to your life, how does it make you feel when you do it God's way? The verse says to do it this way so that you may receive a blessing. We all want to receive a blessing but are we willing to do what it says to get it?

· GIVE FORGIVENESS ·

Luke 6:37-38 (NIV) *³⁷"Do not judge and you will not be judged. Do not condemn, and you will not be condemned.*

Forgive, and you will be forgiven. [38]*Give and it will be given to you. A good measure, pressed down, shaken together and running over, will be poured into your lap. For with the measure you use, it will be measured to you."*

If we don't forgive others we won't be forgiven. Sometimes we feel that so much wrong has been done that it is too much to forgive. However as the verse above states when you forgive much, you will be forgiven much and we all need forgiveness and we need to be forgiven much!

When we choose not to forgive we are hurting ourselves. The person you are not willing to forgive may not care or know that you have not forgiven them. It is most likely not affecting their lives but it is affecting your life. You are the one carrying the load of unforgiveness and it is not an easy load to carry. When you let it go it literally feels like a load has been removed from your life and you become the winner in the situation.

· GIVING MATERIAL THINGS ·

I John 3:16-18 (NIV) [16]*This is how we know what love is: Jesus Christ laid down his life for us. And we ought to lay down our lives for our brothers and sisters.* [17]*If anyone has material possessions and sees a brother or sister in need but has no pity on them, how can the love of God be in that person?* [18]*Dear children, let us not love with words or speech but with actions and in truth.*

Recently I was reading a book and in the book the author was talking about her time with the needy. She was a volunteer at a shelter and when a call for clothing and supplies was sent out some people brought dirty, worn out clothing thinking that it would meet the needs of the poor. Yes it would have given them cover but it did nothing for their dignity. If we cannot give our best who are we to think that we will receive the best from God? We are commanded in scripture over and over again to meet the needs of those who are in need. None of us know when we will be the one in need. We need to put ourselves in the position of the needy and think of them when we give. Treat them as we want to be treated.

I attended the funeral of a dear friend several weeks ago and as I sat and listened to the many stories that were shared of his generous nature I was inspired to be more generous myself. I could see from the people in his life that his generosity had affected many of them and he was greatly blessed for it. One day someone saw him walking home after work so they stopped by to offer him a ride assuming his car had broken down. His car had not broken down but he had just given it someone who needed it more than he did! He gave away a number of cars and one day my mother and I went to meet his wife for lunch and she said she currently does not have a car because her husband gave it away, generosity was a way of life for them and the more they gave away the more God blessed them.

I love the story Robert Morris tells about how he and his wife gave away everything they had including their house and car. If you want to hear a good story about God's abundant giving then you need to read his story. You truly cannot out give God. God does not ask all of us to give away our houses but He does ask us for something. If we refuse to give what He asks then we are limiting the blessing He wants to give us. Again He wants to bless us beyond our imaginations. He owns everything; He has a storehouse we cannot even begin to imagine.

If we give we will receive and not just a little. We will receive a good measure, pressed down, shaken together and running over! That is more than most of us can fathom but God does not lie. The blessing comes with the obedience of giving what we have. The world does not understand this but then we are not living according the worlds rules we live according to Gods laws. He is the one after all who put everything in place, He created the system and He knows what He is talking about. We need to take Him at His word and step out in faith believing what He said is true!

Our faith produces action or at least it should. James tells us about this in the book he authored in the Bible.

James 2:14-17 (NIV) *14What good is it, my brothers and sisters, if someone claims to have faith but has no deeds? Can such faith save them? 15Suppose a brother or a sister is without clothes and daily food. 16If one of you says to them, "Go in peace; keep warm and well fed," but does nothing about their physical needs, what good is it? 17In the same way, faith by itself, if it is not accompanied by action, is dead.*

No matter what we are giving we take the first step in obedience; we show God that we trust His word to be true. We also learn that it truly is more blessed to give than to receive. The joy of giving far outweighs the blessing of receiving. I know that doesn't sound possible to some of you but when you start to give because you want to not because you have to then you will begin to understand this principle. We must meet the needs of those around us, they are our brothers and sisters and we must care for them and share the blessings we have received. Doing this is putting action to our faith that God does bless a cheerful giver.

When we step out in faith our supply will come. We however want proof of the answer before we take the step. I think of the widow in 1 Kings where Elijah asked her to take the last of her meal and make him a cake to eat, all during a famine.

1 Kings 17:10-12 *10So he went to Zarephath. When he came to the town gate, a widow was there gathering sticks. He called*

*to her and asked, "Would you bring me a little water in a jar so
I may have a drink?" ¹¹As she was going to get it, he called, "And
bring me, please, a piece of bread."*

*¹²"As surely as the Lord your God lives," she replied, "I don't
have any bread—only a handful of flour in a jar and a little olive
oil in a jug. I am gathering a few sticks to take home and make a
meal for myself and my son, that we may eat it—and die."*

She stepped out in faith and did as he asked and the meal
and the oil she had did not run out throughout the three year
drought. How many of us would have done that? Would we
have thought things like "who are you that I should feed you
the last of our food?" We may have told him to go elsewhere to
find food. If the widow had done that she and her son would
have died of starvation. God's supply does not run out and He
promises us that if we give we will receive, and not just a little.

2 Corinthians 9:6-7 (NIV) *⁶Remember this: Whoever sows
sparingly will also reap sparingly, and whoever sows generously
will also reap generously. ⁷Each of you should give what you have
decided in your heart to give, not reluctantly or under compulsion,
for God loves a cheerful giver.*

God loves a cheerful giver, are you cheerful when you give?
Do you sow generously? If we believe what the Bible says then
we can see what we should be doing.

· GIVING TITHE ·

Malachi 3:10 (NIV) *¹⁰Bring the whole tithe into the
storehouse, that there may be food in my house. Test me in this,"
says the Lord Almighty, "and see if I will not throw open the
floodgates of heaven and pour out so much blessing that there will
not be room enough to store it.*

This scripture in Malachi is talking about judgment that

comes when we do not give, but this is also before Christ. In the Old Testament they were commanded to give, in the New Testament after Jesus it was no longer a command but a choice. We can choose to give our tithes cheerfully and because we know it pleases our Lord or we can miss the blessing of giving and hoard our money for ourselves. In God's economy the more you give the more you will get. We can look at the above verses again in 2 Corinthians and see that we should give. If you are not interested in being blessed then keep your money or if you give grudgingly then your giving can bless someone else but you should not expect to be blessed, what's in your heart makes the difference.

As far as I know the verses in Malachi are the only time God tells us to test him. This tells us that if we pay our tithe He will throw open the floodgates of heaven and pour out a blessing that we don't have room for. Is there anyone who does not want that kind of a blessing? Yet so many times we think that once we have enough money then we will tithe. If we just had a bit more… but it's never enough. We will not have enough until we give.

Recently I have felt that God is asking me to give more financially. So I have been asking where He would want me to give. I don't want to give where my money is being wasted but rather to a place that I know is meeting the needs of people, teaching God's word and a place where I know people's lives are changing. I have stepped out in faith and committed to several organizations that I believe in and I want to do more. I want to live the blessed life that the Bible talks about. I don't want to go to heaven and then see what I should have been doing and see that I could have made a difference. I want to do all I can with the time I have on this earth and when I pass on to the next life I know that there is a reward for the faithfulness I have shown on earth. I think there is a good chance all of us will get to heaven and see where we could have done so much more with our time on earth.

Tithe is generally thought of as 10% of your income but I have heard a lot about people who give far larger amounts than that. In the scripture above we are told that God will throw open the floodgate of heaven and pour out so much blessing that there will not be room enough to store it. The problem here is that we don't really believe that and because we don't believe it we would never try it because what if it doesn't work?

There are many times we are blessed and we don't really see the blessing. Take for an example your health. If you don't get sick it is a blessing, if your children don't get sick it is a blessing. If you can pay your bills, it is a blessing. We are so blessed and so often take it for granted and do not see what God is doing. Take some time to think about this and maybe even make a list of all the blessing you can think of. You will be amazed at the list you will come up with.

Most of us are familiar with the story in the Bible about the widow who gave the two mites found in Luke.

Luke 21 1-4 (NIV) *¹As Jesus looked up, he saw the rich putting their gifts into the temple treasury. ²He also saw a poor widow put in two very small copper coins. ³"Truly I tell you," he said, "this poor widow has put in more than all the others. ⁴All these people gave their gifts out of their wealth; but she out of her poverty put in all she had to live on."*

When you see this often the question that comes to mind is "what can be done with 2 mites" that is less than one penny. To us the gift looks so small that it seems basically worthless. We see the smallness of the gift but God sees the condition of the heart in which the gift was given. When we give with pride and arrogance because we have lots to give and we want everyone to see our gift we have already received our blessing.

Matthew 6: 1-4 *6"Be careful not to practice your righteousness in front of others to be seen by them. If you do, you will have no reward from your Father in heaven.*

2"So when you give to the needy, do not announce it with trumpets, as the hypocrites do in the synagogues and on the streets, to be honored by others. Truly I tell you, they have received their reward in full. 3But when you give to the needy, do not let your left hand know what your right hand is doing, 4so that your giving may be in secret. Then your Father, who sees what is done in secret, will reward you.

Jesus was comparing the giving practices of the righteous Jews and their pride in being seen in their giving with the right way to give. Give in secret. If you have never done this you really need to. I cannot describe the joy you receive from giving in secret. This type of giving is often given above and beyond your tithe which is generally given to your church or ministry where you are being fed.

An offering is the extra you give as a blessing to others. There is also a first fruits offering. On occasion when I am traveling through Atlanta I visit a large church that I enjoy in the area. Every Sunday morning they give an opportunity for those who have received an increase that past week to give a first fruits offering. Members of the congregation will walk to the front a place their first fruits offering on the altar.

What do we do when we have an increase in pay or receive a bonus? Do we think about giving some to God? Can we do it cheerfully?

2 Corinthians 9:7 (NIV) *7Each of you should give what*

you have decided in your heart to give, not reluctantly or under compulsion, for God loves a cheerful giver.

Let's check our attitude the next time we are giving our tithe or offerings. If you give because you feel you have to then it is time that you learn to give because you want to, because you love God and you love His people.

11

Love One Another

· LOVE ONE ANOTHER THAT
YOUR JOY MAY BE FULL ·

L ove must be sincere

How does sincere love look? I looked up some information to get a clear understanding of what this looks like.

· Genuine in feeling, she offered a sincere apology for her angry outburst

Synonyms heartfelt, unfeigned

· Related Words honest, translucent, transparent, true; authentic, genuine; hearty, wholehearted

· Free from any intent to deceive or impress others, done out of a sincere desire to help others.

We have all seen someone mistreat someone they say they love. When your love is sincere it shows. Sometimes we can see love in someone's eyes, it is heartfelt and moving. Let's make sure that our love is sincere. I believe it is sincere love that changes people. We are told that love never fails; let's make sure we are sincere in our loving of others.

Most Christians know that the thirteenth chapter of 1 Corinthians is known as the love chapter. In it we can see that no matter what gift we have been given if we do not have love our gift is worth nothing.

1 Corinthians 13:1-3 (NIV) *¹If I speak in the tongues of men or of angels, but do not have love, I am only a resounding gong or a clanging cymbal. ²If I have the gift of prophecy and can fathom all mysteries and all knowledge, and if I have a faith that can move mountains, but do not have love, I am nothing. ³If I give all I possess to the poor and give over my body to hardship that I may boast, but do not have love, I gain nothing.*

I believe that most Christians want to be used and want at least one of these spiritual gifts. We want to have purpose in life, to fulfill our calling, but the gift is worthless if you do not first love people. Not all people are easy to love and we have to push through our feelings and learn to love all people. God loves all people, He does not choose which ones to love, and He is the Father of everyone alive. If we can remember this and learn to see others the way God does we can also learn to love other people.

The portion of scripture goes on to tell us what love is.

1 Corinthians 13:4-8 (NIV) *⁴Love is patient, love is kind. It does not envy, it does not boast, it is not proud. ⁵It does not dishonor others, it is not self-seeking, it is not easily angered, it keeps no record of wrongs. ⁶Love does not delight in evil but rejoices with the truth. ⁷It always protects, always trusts, always hopes, always perseveres.*

⁸Love never fails.

We have a tendency to think that if we point out the bad things others are doing it will make them want to repent and turn to God but according to this it is love that brings change, it never fails.

Let's take a further look at parts of these scriptures.

· LOVE IS PATIENT ·

Well right there I probably lost some of you. Patience is not easy but as I mentioned earlier in this book we desperately need patience and one way or another we will learn to be patient.

Romans 12:11 has one little phrase in it about patience that paints another look at being patient.

¹¹Be patient in affliction!

Are you kidding me! Patience is not something that most of us have a lot of but it is something we all need in our lives. I have recently been looking at the life of Elijah. I imagine being by the brook being fed by ravens and I picture myself in that situation and I don't see myself being joyful or patient.

When we are suffering we are asked to be patient. None of us enjoys suffering. We want it to be over and over now, not later. We might be suffering through sickness or suffering from loss of a loved one or the loss of a job. Regardless we are asked to be patient. I suppose if we can learn to be patient under these circumstances we can learn to be patient in most things. The next time you find yourself in a situation of suffering remember that patience is what is required. I think if we would practice some of these things we would learn a lot from them. When God asks something of us there is always a good reason for it. Unless we follow what is asked of us we will never understand the reason it is asked. Patience in suffering just might teach us something valuable, let's put it to practice and see what we learn. We are all surrounded by people who are suffering from one thing or another. We have the opportunity to be a word of cheer and encouragement. When we show that we care and we show the love of God we can see their spirits lifted. We can bring hope for a good outcome to their circumstances and a better future, in the process we will also learn something of great value.

· LOVE DOES NOT ENVY, IT DOES NOT BOAST, IT IS NOT PROUD ·

Envy is rampant in our society. People look at what others have and they want to outdo them and have even more. Cell phones are a good example of this. When a new phone comes out and our friend gets it we have to have it too. If we don't get the new phone we feel "less than" and we need to keep up with the Jones'. We need to grow up and learn to be happy with what we have. There is nothing wrong with having things but when our motive is envy, or we boast about everything we have and show off with pride then there is a big problem.

· LOVE KEEPS NO RECORD OF WRONGS ·

This is another area where we tend to fail. If we truly love people then we let issues go, we do not hang on looking for a chance to get even or repay. We forget the wrongs that have been done and we move on. If you can accomplish this you will have overcome a big problem.

· LOVE ALWAYS PROTECTS ·

A mother will protect the child she loves; we need to do the same with others. How does this look in real life? Several months ago while I was watching a program on TV I saw a gentleman who was asking people on the street the question "If your dog and a stranger were both drowning and you could save only one which one would you save?" I was appalled to see that many of the people said "my dog". How is this even possible? When you don't believe in God and you think only of yourself this is who you can become. People were choosing to protect the dog over a human!

Life is a blessing and we need to value not only our own

life but also the lives of others. We need to look out for each other and genuinely care for others. The story above is the way some people look at life, how they value life. On the other hand we hear stories of people who risk their lives trying to save a total stranger.

Some time back I met a very nice young man who told me his story. He was a pizza delivery man and as he was delivering pizza he saw a car go into a pond with two people in it. He stopped his car and dove into the water to try to save the people. He did all he could but he could not save them. He risked his life for total strangers.

What a difference in these two examples, one values life and protects others; the other has no compassion for others.

Protecting others can also be in not spreading rumors or in defending others when they hear gossip. We can put the end to the things people are saying about others by just defending the person, protecting them with positive words that we can speak. We need to love others and always look for ways to protect them from whatever situations we can, this shows the love of God.

· LOVE ALWAYS PERSEVERES ·

Love does not give up! When you love someone who is not living a Christian life you do not give up on them, you love them until their eyes are opened and they see truth. Truth will set them free but your love will lead the way. No one wins anyone over with ridicule and hatred.

This doesn't mean that persevering love is always easy.

We as a family have had a wonderful opportunity to persevere in love in a situation that many would have chosen differently. Our son left his wife and children and moved to a city several hours away. A divorce followed and our daughter-in-law and three grandchildren were left on their own. We got involved as a family to help with the children and to love on our daughter-in-law. We supported her in every way that we could and still do. For several years she struggled to reestablish a life for herself and our grandchildren. Our hearts were broken and we so wanted the marriage to survive but it didn't.

In time she met a very nice young man and remarried. I cannot say it was an easy time for me but on the other hand I knew she wanted to be married, she wanted security for herself as well as her children. She wanted to be loved and appreciated. I struggled with it for a short period of time but then I noticed something that changed everything.

My grandson was smiling again! How could I not love a man that put a smile on my grandsons face? The children began to heal and I could tell they were settling into a normal family life again. This wonderful young man brought healing to this hurting family. We included them in our family gatherings, birthday parties and picnics. We got to know him. Our daughters and daughter-in -law maintained their friendship throughout the entire ordeal. But still there were times that were hard.

I have always tried to attend the games, recitals, musicals and whatever else my grandchildren are involved in. One summer evening I went to my granddaughter's baseball game and I sat with our daughter-in-law and her new husband. He got a phone call and the person calling wanted to meet with him in a few minutes. I couldn't help but overhear his side of the conversation as I sat beside him. He explained to the person on the other end "I cannot come right now; I am at my little girl's baseball game."

Everything in me wanted to get up and shout "She is not

your little girl!" but I knew in reality she was his little girl. He was the one who tucked her in at night, he was the one who was taking her to church and teaching her about God's love for her and he was the one at her ball game cheering her on, he was in all respects her "dad" and she was his "little girl."

Today he is as much our son-in-law as she is our daughter-in-law. We love them both and are so thankful for what he has done for this precious family. When we see each other in public or private we are family and we treat each other as family.

I imagine that there are people in our community that just don't believe that this is real, but it is. As I think about it I pray that the decision we made to love our daughter-in-law and to include her still in our family shows the love of Jesus to those around us.

Other families may choose to blame their daughter-in-law for what happened; they may choose to fight and belittle her and in the process hurt their grandchildren. For us as a family that wasn't even an option. They had been hurt enough without us adding to their pain. Instead we chose to love and accept her and her new husband into our family. We love our son and he is always invited to every gathering we have but if he chooses not to come then our daughter and son-in-law know they are always welcome. To some people this may seem like the hard thing to do, to us it was the right thing to do. Loving the man in her life is so much easier than hating, blaming and fighting. There is peace in doing what is right. Love heals a lot of pain.

Although our son is not living for God at this time we love him. I learned early in this battle that trying to talk him into the Kingdom wasn't working so I decided to try it Gods way. All of us as a family love him and want to see him live a godly life; we are waiting for the day when truth will be seen, what a glorious day that will be for all of us! Our love will persevere because we know that love never fails!

In Romans chapter 12 we read that we should be devoted to one another in love.

When you truly love someone it is not hard to be devoted to them. People who love each other never intentionally hurt one another; they are kind and gentle and care more about the other person than themselves. When you love one another with devotion you look out for the other person, their joy becomes your joy and their sorrow becomes your sorrow. You go out of your way to make sure that they are taken care of and their needs are met. That is how God loves us.

Once we get to the point that we understand the Fathers love we can relax because we know He is taking care of our needs. We worship Him because we are devoted to Him; He takes care of us because He loves us.

Humans loving humans can be quite different. It shouldn't be but it is. We don't trust each other so it is hard to be devoted, we are afraid of being hurt so we are not devoted to a relationship. Couples decide not to get married and will just live together thinking they can't get hurt that way. Any time that you have a relationship with another person you risk getting hurt but without that committed love for one another you never have a truly bonding of two hearts.

We don't see very much of this truly devoted love in our world. Our world is full of a "me first" kind of love. I will do for you if you will do for me, kind of love. It seems as though everyone is looking out for themselves and most relationships are looked at as a period of time, "as long as it lasts" relationship. People choose to live together instead of getting married because they are afraid of a long time commitment. They do not love each other with true devotion.

I will have to admit that it can be scary to completely trust someone else with your best interest. They have the opportunity to hurt us. I suppose many people have been hurt or have seen their loved ones hurt and it scares them so they think they are protecting themselves by not getting married and making a lifetime commitment.

We live in a world of imperfect people. We do have to make wise choices. I have talked to my granddaughters and encouraged them to be careful about who they date. It is easy to fall in lover when you are young and once you fall for someone you generally don't think very clearly. I have encouraged them to not even date someone who they wouldn't marry.

Devoted love isn't just for married folks. There are some truly deeply devoted friendships that last a life time. I have a very dear friend who I have known all my life. I trust her with my deepest secrets. We seldom see each other these days but whenever we get together we can pick up right where we left off the last time. I trust her to the point that if she heard a rumor about me she would defend me without having to talk to me first. I would do the same for her. I know her and I would always defend her. We are devoted to each other. That feels good. Everyone should have friends like this, I am blessed.

The love that we as humans have for each other isn't perfect. Sometimes we fail at loving others but God always loves, as a matter of fact God is love! Paul tries to get us to see this and understand this love in a letter to the Ephesians.

Ephesians 3:17-21 (NIV) *17I pray that you, being rooted and established in love, 18may have power, together with all the Lord's holy people, to grasp how wide and long and high and deep is the* *love of Christ, ¹⁹and to know this love that surpasses knowledge—that you may be filled to the measure of all the fullness of God.*

²⁰Now to him who is able to do immeasurably more than all we ask or imagine, according to his power that is at work within us, ²¹to him be glory in the church and in Christ Jesus throughout all generations, forever and ever! Amen.

How would our lives be different if we got a hold of this truth of God's love for us? There is so much for us to learn on this subject and the Bible is full of the love of God. We can see God's love throughout scripture in how He has taken care of the people like Moses, Abraham and Elijah in the old testament and we can see it in the life of Jesus as he came and showed love and compassion to those He met.

God loves us just as He did the people we read about in the Bible; all of us are part of His plan, His good plan for life. He takes care of us, He talks to us and He provides for us, these are all things we do in the natural for our loved ones and God loves us even more than we love our own families.

12

Instructions for Godly Living

· WALK IN THE WAY OF LOVE ·

As a new Christian we often come into the kingdom with little knowledge of how to live. The Bible is new to us and many people have heard others say that the Bible is outdated and not relevant for today. This is a lie from Satan. The Bible never loses its power or its message. It is just as relevant today as it was two thousand years ago. When we live according to Gods plan our lives reflect Him, we love and treat others the way He instructs us to.

Of course it is not only new Christians that need to know how to live a godly life, all of us need to be reminded and we need to read and meditate on what our lives should look like.

In Romans we find a great message of what our lives should look like from the words of Paul.

Romans 12:9-21(NIV) *⁹Love must be sincere. Hate what is evil; cling to what is good. ¹⁰Be devoted to one another in love. Honor one another above yourselves. ¹¹Never be lacking in zeal, but keep your spiritual fervor, serving the Lord. ¹²Be joyful in hope, patient in affliction, faithful in prayer. [13] Share with the Lord's people who are in need. Practice hospitality.*

[14] Bless those who persecute you; bless and do not curse. [15] Rejoice with those who rejoice; mourn with those who mourn. [16] Live in harmony with one another. Do not be proud, but be willing to associate with people of low position. Do not be conceited.

[17] Do not repay anyone evil for evil. Be careful to do what is right in the eyes of everyone. [18] If it is possible, as far as it depends on you, live at peace with everyone. [19] Do not take revenge, my dear friends, but leave room for God's wrath, for it is written: "It is mine to avenge; I will repay," says the Lord. [20] On the contrary:

"If your enemy is hungry, feed him;

if he is thirsty, give him something to drink.

In doing this, you will heap burning coals on his head."

[21] Do not be overcome by evil, but overcome evil with good.

These verses on how we should live and love are amazing. When we see what love really looks like we see quickly how far we fall short of what God wants from us.

· HATE WHAT IS EVIL ·

When you see evil things happen you should have this sickening feeling in the pit of your stomach. We have all felt it. We see an injustice done towards someone and it makes us sick. All evil comes from one place, the devil. He is the very essence of evil. He will do everything he can to destroy lives, to bring disaster and he is full of hate especially for those of us who love and worship God. In saying this let us also remember that God who lives within us is far greater than Satan. He has overcome Satan and so have we, we just need to know it.

When we see evil being done we need to do our part to overcome evil with good. There are ways to fight against evil and the best way is to do good where you see evil occur.

Romans 12:21 (NIV) *²¹Do not be overcome by evil, but overcome evil with good. Cling to what is good.*

Good things, the thought of clinging to what is good is calming. Recently one of my granddaughters was telling me about a rather rude comment that someone made to her and she was feeling rather down and out about it. I told her that I was writing a book about controlling your mind and not thinking on things that you don't need or shouldn't be thinking about. I told her that her thoughts are under her control and she does not have to think about what was said. The thought of it made her sad and hopefully she learned something of value from her Nana.

Choosing to think about things that are good, things that bring a smile to your face as well as God's will always bring stress relief. We get all stressed about things because we are not thinking or clinging to what is good. There is a lot of good in our lives that we tend to overlook. For some reason it seems to be easier to think about the bad things that happen to us rather than the good things. When someone is rude to us we carry it with us and it outweighs the good things that others have done for us and we need to reverse this bad habit.

We all love good things, we love it when it is working in our lives and we love it when good things happen to those we love and care about. When your mind wants to go to the negative things in life stop yourself and remind yourself that there are good things to think about and then cling to those thoughts.

· HONOR ONE ANOTHER ABOVE YOURSELF ·

To honor one another above ourselves is a selfless act and shows our love for others. Do we really want to allow the other person to enjoy the praise for something done well? We are so hungry for recognition that we will often take credit for something that we really didn't do or we may have had a small part in. We overlook others who helped and take the credit for ourselves because we are so hungry for praise. There is something wrong in our world when we act like this. Try sitting back and letting the other person shine in the spot light.

I saw this so often in my father. There were many times that others were praised for things that he was involved with or things that succeeded because of his involvement and he was happy for them and was content to sit in the background allowing others to receive the credit. He loved watching others be promoted and recognized because he loved people and he believed in others. He helped many people succeed and sometime it cost him a large sum of money that was never repaid. He allowed God to take it and let it go. He was excellent in allowing others to be honored above himself.

· NEVER BE LACKING IN ZEAL BUT KEEP YOUR SPIRITUAL FERVOR ·

I love this thought. We are all guilty of being on fire for God at times and then growing cold at other times. I have found that when I am facing hard circumstances I dig into my relationship with God the most. This realization makes my mind go all kinds of places. First, is it possible that I would face less hard circumstances if I kept my zeal for God? Is it possible that God allows hard circumstances so that I will keep my zeal? Second, why wouldn't I just keep my zeal and avoid the tough circumstances? I will probably never know the answer to this but one fact remains; no matter where my faith is God's love for me never changes.

I have at times prayed that God would never let me forget the times of closeness I experience with Him and that my life would never feel so complete without Him that I forget about Him. It seems that when everything in life is good it is easier to forget about a relationship with God. I talk to God throughout the day and often find myself talking to God thanking Him for a beautiful sunset or asking Him to help me remember something. Constant communication is the key to having and keeping your zeal for the Lord.

· BE JOYFUL IN HOPE ·

Sometimes all we have is hope for something better. We have situations in our families, in our jobs and we live with the hope that things will get better. When things are not as we would like them to be can we be joyful or do we complain till everyone around us is sick of hearing us? We are to be joyful while we are hoping for change. There is hope! The God I serve allows me to always have hope. He gives me reason to hope. I read His Word and I see reason for hope. There are situations in my own life that I am waiting for, I am hoping for the answer to come and I certainly would not have been disappointed had the answer arrived before now but I still have hope and I know I have good reason to hope. Meanwhile I am joyful. My hope is in God and He will never fail me. The joy of the Lord is my strength. Give hope to others and be a source of joy in their lives. Show your love for those around you and joy will follow.

· BE FAITHFUL IN PRAYER ·

As I look at this I have two thoughts. I need to be faithful and pray, talk to my Father, and I need to have faith when I pray, believing that what I ask for in the Fathers' name I will receive. I think both of these are equally important.

Being faithful to pray and being in constant communication with the Lord is what helps us live a good and peaceful life. It is what builds our communication with our Creator. We need to pray when we have a need, feel a burden for someone or something but also be thankful for how God has blessed us and thank Him for things that He has created and provided for us. Having a thankful and merry heart is like good medicine.

Proverbs 17:22 (NIV)

22A cheerful heart is good medicine,
but a crushed spirit dries up the bones.

Proverbs 17:22 (MSG)

22A cheerful disposition is good for your health;
gloom and doom leave you bone-tired.

This translation in the Message Bible tells us how tiring gloom and doom are. We need to think on the good things in life and learn to be thankful and cheerful. God loves to see his children happy and cheerful and when we talk to God we need to come to Him with this attitude. God understands that we will go through hard times and it is easy for us to become sad and burdened and we may come to Him with a load of problems but it is His desire to see us overcome our problems and be cheerful and happy, much like we want our own children to be.

Then again we give thanks for the simple reason that God is good!

Psalm 118:1

1Give thanks to the Lord, for he is good;
his love endures forever.

You can also look at "be faithful in prayer" as having faith when you pray, expecting God to answer your prayers.

John 14:13-14 (NIV) *13I will do whatever you ask in my*

name, so that the Father may be glorified in the Son. [14]You may ask me for anything in my name, and I will do it.

This does not give us a license to ask for things that are against God's will. We need to know and understand Gods will in a situation before we ask. Sometimes we pray because we want something but we also need to know that God knows more about our needs than we do and He knows what is best for us. Have any of your children ever asked you for something that you knew was not a good idea for them, or that you knew would cause a problem for them and you said "no"? If so then you can understand that God as a Father is no different. You can also know that God wants to answer our prayers and often we just don't ask with the right motives or we fail to ask at all. When you go to God in prayer go to Him understanding all of this and give thanks and expect that God knows what is best. God will always do what is best for you!

· SHARE WITH THE LORDS' PEOPLE WHO ARE IN NEED ·

Americans are known the world over as people who help the needy in various parts of the world. We have hundreds of charities to support and many churches offer the opportunity to go on mission trips where we can see firsthand the needs of others. Giving to the poor is one of the things that highly pleases the Lord. When we support ministries and take missions trips to help others we are sharing with those in need. In the end we will find a joy in the fact that we made a difference in the lives of people that God loves just as much as He loves us.

Matthew 10:42 (NIV) *[42]And if anyone gives even a cup of cold water to one of these little ones who is my disciple, truly I tell you, that person will certainly not lose their reward*

When we share a cup of water with the thirsty God will reward us. There will always be poor people around us and we can always give something. I have often heard it said that the people who have the least are the most willing to share what they have. I think we can so often get familiar with the poverty around us that we don't see it any more. We think that our giving to the poor has to be in a third world country. Sharing with those who are in need includes that single mom down the street, the widow you see at the grocery store and the fatherless children in your children's classroom at school.

When I think of the poor people around the world I cannot help but remember the story I heard from a lady in our church who was traveling in a poor country and a lady who had nothing offered her only cooking pan to her. She was willing to give all she had to the visitor. We are often not willing to give out of our abundance.

James 1:27 (NIV) *27Religion that God our Father accepts as pure and faultless is this: to look after orphans and widows in their distress and to keep oneself from being polluted by the world.*

If we open our eyes we will find many people who we can help. We will be blessed when we do and it will please the Father. Find an orphanage or a homeless shelter where you can either donate time or money or both.

One of the last things I told my father before he passed away was that he does not need to worry about mom; I would take care of her. I have gone out of my way to spend time with her, to take her places and make sure she gets out of the house. She is a home body but I recognize that she needs to get out, be around people and keep moving. Not all widows have children living nearby to help take care of them and we need to be aware of who these widows are and meet their needs, that is part of what the church is called to do. Taking care of the needs of others is love.

· PRACTICE HOSPITALITY ·

There are some people who have a gift of hospitality. They go out of their way to invite guests, prepare meals and make others feel welcome. Then are those like me that have to practice hospitality. When I say practice I seriously mean practice. It is not natural for me. Take for an example my friend Kathy who not only invites guests to her house, prepares a meal but she even uses real dishes! I might invite you over but we may eat off of paper plates.

I have been working on this and am putting forth efforts to invite guests to our home. Easter is coming up and my children and grandchildren are all coming for dinner. I also invited my widowed aunt and my mother to come as well as a few others who I thought may not have anyone to spend the holiday with. I have been becoming more aware that there are many people who are alone for holidays and I try to put myself in their positions, how would it feel to be alone when everyone around you is gathering for a holiday with family? Yes, I am practicing; I plan to get better at this.

· BLESS THOSE WHO PERSECUTE YOU ·

Wow can you really bless those who persecute you? Is that really possible? It is only possible if we allow God to be God. My mind goes to all the Christians that have been beheaded by groups such as ISIS. What does it take to be able to bless those kinds of people? Then I remember Jesus on the cross saying "forgive them for they know not what they are doing." That is the picture of perfection. Bless and do not curse, that happens only with God and with the understanding we get from having a relationship with the Lord.

Many of us have never faced persecution anywhere near this extreme yet we have a hard time blessing someone who does us a slight injustice. If you have ever had someone lie about you and spread false rumors that have hurt you or your family members that you love then you know that feeling that rises up inside you that wants to take care of it. It takes the power of the Holy Spirit to be able to bless a person who has hurt you or those you love. Yet that is what we are called to do. When we bless and do not curse, we are showing the love of Jesus.

· REJOICE WITH THOSE WHO REJOICE, MOURN WITH THOSE WHO MOURN ·

When we rejoice because of the good things in our lives we want others to rejoice with us. We are excited and we want others to be excited for us. We need to learn to do that for those around us. Many times instead of rejoicing with other people we tend to be too jealous to rejoice for them. How wonderful would it be if we could learn to be genuinely happy for the success of others! There would be so much to celebrate if we could celebrate other people's good times. Rejoicing feels good, it is uplifting; it is invigorating and brings with it a positive air that lifts everyone's spirits. Genuinely rejoicing for and with others shows the love we have for each other and love never fails. Let's learn to rejoice, it's a party!

On the other hand we also need to mourn with others when they are mourning. During a time of mourning we need the comfort of others. Often we feel that we have to say something to make things better but most times it is better to just be there offering a shoulder to cry on and doing simple things like running errands, taking phone calls, or just sitting with those who are suffering. So many times in our desire to say something we say the wrong thing. We don't mean for it to come out wrong but it tends to end up that way. I remember being with a close relative at the time of the loss of her husband of only a few weeks. Standing next to her I was there when a gentleman came up and said "I know just how you feel, my sister lost her husband last year." This poor young lady turned to me and said "that is not the same, he has no idea how I feel!" I hugged her and assured her that he does not; it really was not the same. Many times saying nothing is better than trying to bring comfort with the wrong words. When others are mourning, the love we show is like a fresh spring rain, it brings hope for the future.

· LIVE IN HARMONY WITH ONE ANOTHER ·

This alone would change the world we live in. People cannot get along, everyone has to be right and everyone is easily offended. People declare their rights and look for ways to take offense at innocent words that are spoken. If there is any way that the words we say can be heard wrong and used to create a battle it is done. People don't want to get along, they want to fight and many have no idea how wonderful harmony is.

When I think of harmony I cannot help but think of music. I love to hear people sing in harmony it is a beautiful sound. One voice blended with another to bring a melody to my ears is one of my favorite things and I never tire of it. I love good singing and good music. I have four young granddaughters who are learning to sing in harmony and I could listen to them sing for hours. Harmony is a beautiful thing whether it is in song or in relationships.

I have many employees and one thing I enforce at all of our businesses is that people get along. No one likes to work at a job that is full of personal agendas and gossip. I will not tolerate it. I am not asking two people to live together, I am asking them to get along a day at work. The atmosphere is so much more pleasant when there is harmony. I don't want my employees to bring their personal problems to work with them and I don't want them to take their work life home either. If you can eliminate gossip and back biting at work it is much easier to go home and forget about work. Everyone should be able to have these two worlds in their lives and keep them separate. It is when there is stress and tension at work that it is hard to leave it at work.

We have to learn to get along with others. When we learn that we don't always have to have the last word that we don't always have to be right we welcome harmony. We also learn it really doesn't matter who is right. What is right is far more important than who is right. Drop it, let it go, get over your differences and get along. Life is meant to be good and it is far to short to spend it fighting about everything. We need to learn not to make everything personal.

I get very frustrated when I am watching people talk on television and a person gets all riled up and offended about something that is said that was not meant to be in any way taken the way they are interpreting it. They are just looking for a fight and are not happy unless they can create a hostile environment. It is one of the reasons I watch very little TV, I don't need that junk in my life.

· DO NOT BE PROUD BUT ASSOCIATE WITH PEOPLE OF LOW POSITION ·

Why do we put people into categories, what is the point? When God looks on humanity He does not think more of one person than He does another. He loves all of us equally. He loves the believer and the unbeliever. He died for all of us. We need to realize that we are neither above others nor below others. We may have a job or title that gives us power over others but that is not a license to treat people unfairly. A title should not make us proud; we are not going to take that title to heaven with us. When we stand before God He is not going to say that your title as president of the company is going to get you a bigger mansion in heaven. It will make no difference. What will make a difference is how you treated others. Were you proud and haughty and did you mistreat Gods people? Did you love as Jesus loved and treat everyone fairly? Do not be proud, it is ugly!

· DO NOT BE CONCEITED ·

Conceited is having too high an opinion of oneself, sounds a lot like pride.

Just look at these words that describe being conceited; pompous, prideful, proud, self-conceited, self-important, self-opinionated, self-satisfied, smug, stuck-up, swellheaded, vain. Notice a lot of "self" words. We can become so self important that we look down our long noses at others and think we are so much better than they are. Who do we think we are? God must look down and shake His head at times.

For some reason Hollywood has been able to build a wall that separates the "beautiful people" from the rest of us. They as a whole seem to think that their opinion carries more weight and is worth more than anyone else's. I saw this to be true in the last election. Sometimes I would watch as some of these so called "stars" would get up in front of crowds and sway the masses with their views causing more division in an already divided country. They often are self-opinionated and smug, or conceited.

We have to be careful because it is very easy to become like this. When we have some success in life we can quickly start thinking a bit too highly of ourselves and become conceited. We have to continually remind ourselves of who we are in Christ and keep our heads out of the clouds of pride.

· DO NOT REPAY ANYONE EVIL FOR EVIL ·

Anger is a strong force but anger in itself is not wrong. Turning the other cheek goes against our human nature and is another area where we have to learn to think differently. When we get angry we want to retaliate, we want to make them pay for what they did or said. That however is not how we are to react. We are to remember that God says "It is mine to avenge, I will repay" but our responsibility in this is to feed our enemy, give him a drink if he is thirsty and let God take it from there. In other words, show love and keep your hands off and let God be God.

When I think of the crucifixion of Christ and how He just took the beatings, the mockery and punishment when He had done nothing wrong it makes me think of how many small things I have had done to me that I felt I needed to get even for. I want to even the score and be on top, it is what we all want by our human nature. Yet Jesus turned the other cheek and allowed Himself to be mocked without so much as a word to His own defense. How hard would that be to do and to think that all of this was done to the Son of God? I think about the sky turning dark, the curtain in the temple being torn in two, and the dead people who came back to life during this time. Surely those who crucified Christ must have realized that Jesus was no ordinary man. I wonder did they start to think about the fact that they may have been wrong, maybe He really was the son of God? How would I have felt to think that maybe you had just crucified the Son of God? Was there fear of retaliation from God for what they had done?

Matthew 5:38-40 (NIV) *38"You have heard that it was said, 'Eye for eye, and tooth for tooth.' 39But I tell you, do not resist an evil person. If anyone slaps you on the right cheek, turn to them the other cheek also. 40And if anyone wants to sue you and take your shirt, hand over your coat as well.*

How do we show love when we are mistreated? We are told in scripture that love never fails. When we turn the other cheek and are not looking to even the score but humble ourselves we are showing the world what Christianity looks like. Many people have seen Christians who didn't show much love but rather condemning Christians who do nothing but shout hell fire and brimstone. Scaring people into Christianity was not what we were instructed to do.

When we learn to control our tempers and not retaliate or take it upon ourselves to "make them pay" but allow God to take care of the injustice then we are doing it the way God intended. This is far beyond our human ability it is the Holy Spirit that helps us show love when we cannot do it on our own.

All of our lives we have looked at it wrong, it was our duty to get even, to teach them a lesson. Now we are called to completely change our ways. Once we follow these instructions we start seeing how it all works. It is a better way. There is peace in letting it go. It is easier to move on to other things and forget the past if we just allow God to do His thing and we move on to do other things. So much less stress! Who doesn't need less stress in this busy world? We have enough to deal with in everyday life without having to even all the scores and keep track of who did what and who is still on the list that we need to deal with. How much easier is life Gods way? God did not put burdens on us and make us responsible to deal with these issues; He will take care of it. No one outruns God.

· DO NOT BE OVERCOME WITH EVIL BUT OVERCOME EVIL WITH GOOD ·

What a goal! There is evil all around us but we are change agents: we have the answer to a better life. Good over comes evil! I am writing this at a time when we are seeing police officers being shot in various cities in the United States. Evil is so prevalent and yet good is also found. Just this week as I watching some of the convention taking place in Cleveland Ohio I saw a scene where three African Americans went up to a white police officer and prayed with him, they all gave him a hug and thanked him for doing a good job. It was a beautiful scene and made me smile to see good overcome evil. We can all do our part. The world is full of evil which gives us many opportunities to overcome evil! Look around you and do something good where you see evil happening. Light and dark cannot co-exist. This is a wonderful challenge for all of us because we all have the opportunity to be involved in overcoming evil and it is not hard to do. Make it a challenge to yourself that you will do something to overcome evil when you see it. You don't have to see evil to do good; good always makes a difference. We can have a better world by all doing good every chance we get.

The right answer is always to love one another.

13

Where Does God Fit Into the Equation?

· SEEK YE FIRST THE KINGDOM OF GOD
AND HIS RIGHTEOUSNESS, AND ALL THESE
THINGS SHALL BE ADDED UNTO YOU ·

I remember as a child learning a little ditty that taught me how to love Jesus.

"JOY - Jesus first, yourself last and others in between" This pretty well says it all. We are to love Jesus/God first and foremost. It seems that today people tend to love themselves first, others next and if they have time for God they might give him a minute or two each day. That is not how to love God.

Matthew 22:37 (NIV) *37 Jesus replied: "'Love the Lord your God with all your heart and with all your soul and with all your mind.'*

Not many of us can truthfully say that we love God like this. Are we even capable of loving God in this way? I personally think this should be our aim. God knows what we are capable of as humans and I believe that this should be what we set as our goal. God knows our hearts and He knows if we are trying to fulfill this or not. We can say whatever we want but He knows the truth, He knows every thought we have and nothing is hidden from Him. Isn't it strange that we think we can hide our motives from God?

God wants our undivided attention, He wants to be first in our lives, and He wants to be praised and worshiped. When we realize all that He has done for us we want to live up to these expectations. We must however put effort into making this happen. It is very easy to get busy with life and days go by without spending time with Him and praising Him for everything He has provided for us. We need to worship and adore Him regardless of what else is going on in our lives. In other words we have to do it on purpose. We need to start our day with Him, in His Word, talking to Him inviting Him to be with us and letting Him know that He is welcome in our lives. It is called a sacrifice of praise for a reason. There are many times when we just don't feel like praising. Maybe we have had a long day at work or if you are like me I am so busy at work and I am often surrounded by people all day, I love to go home and just enjoy the quiet. I don't always feel like praising. I have learned though that when I make the effort and I start singing to the Lord it lifts my spirit and I am refreshed.

I remember my dad talking about inviting God to travel with him. At one point in life he was alone on the road a lot. There were numerous times when he would pull his car up along the side of the road and reach over to open the passenger door and invite God to travel with him. This was a deliberate action, an action of inviting God into his life. He was communicating with God about everyday life, we may call it prayer, and we are told to pray without ceasing.

Prayer without ceasing, I believe this is done simply by talking to God throughout the day. He wants to hear from us, He wants us to see what He is doing for us throughout our day. We need to learn to recognize the things He works out for our good. How many times do we stop to thank Him for a day that is going so well, or a safe drive we may have dreaded? Good things are happening all the time and we think it's just coincidence, no God is at work in our lives and we need to see it!

On the other hand if things seem to be going wrong all day we need to stop and take time for God. We need to ask Him to intervene in our day to make it run smoothly. Then we need to thank Him and expect things to turn around.

As you spend time in the word of God or praising Him, communicating with Him and getting to know your Savior you develop a relationship with Him. You learn to understand what He wants for your life and how much He loves you. You start to see that without Him there is no hope for your future. Those who know Him personally have no desire to be without Him. He is a priority in their lives. They hear from Him and they know His voice. For myself I cannot imagine trying to live life without God. Life is too hard to go it alone. The very idea of having to do it alone is overwhelming to me and I have no desire to live without Him.

Recently I had the opportunity to pray with a wonderful lady who was going through a very hard time. As parents we so desperately want our grown children to make good and godly choices. But they are adults and we cannot make their choices for them. We watch them make bad choices and we know where it will lead. No matter how hard we try to help them see the error of their choices they do not always listen. When that happens as it did in this case it can be devastating. I know how it feels, I've been there. I encouraged this dear lady to trust God and let Him take the load. There is nothing she can do but she has the Lord who is able to do anything. In order to have peace she has to be able to give it to God. The better you know God the easier it is to give it to Him and trust Him with it. Knowing what the Word of God says about our children gives us promises we can stand on when things get hard. In the end it's the adult child's choice but we pray that God will send someone into their lives that will speak life to them or that God will remind them of things they were taught and we pray for them to make the right choices. This is just one of the many times we need to learn to depend on God. It is hard to depend on someone you do not know.

Our lives are of full of trouble; dishonesty abounds and seems to be the norm. If it feels good do it and so much more. We need God! Our country needs God!

God has forgiven so much and He's welcomed us to be His followers. The grace of God is amazing. I don't believe that we really get it. I hear arguments about the grace of God because people think that grace and unconditional forgiveness gives people a license to sin. That is not how a person who truly understands grace feels or thinks. How can you want to sin against a God when He has so freely given us so much? I can choose to sin and I know I am forgiven but when I sin I have given Satan inroads to my life. I cannot live in victory if I allow Satan to have access to my life. Why would I want to do that, why would any of us choose to do that? Understanding God's grace does not make me want to go out and sin against Him, it makes me want to worship Him.

If I have accepted Christ as my Savior then there is no condemnation, I am free!

Romans 8:1-2 (NIV) *¹Therefore, there is now no condemnation for those who are in Christ Jesus, ²because through Christ Jesus the law of the Spirit who gives life has set you free from the law of sin and death.*

Romans 8:31-39 (NIV) *31If God is for us, who can be against us? 32He who did not spare His own Son, but gave Him up for us all—how will He not also, along with Him, graciously give us all things? 33Who will bring any charge against those whom God has chosen? It is God who justifies. 34Who then is the one who condemns? No one. Christ Jesus who died—more than that, who was raised to life—is at the right hand of God and is also interceding for us. 35Who shall separate us from the love of Christ? Shall trouble or hardship or persecution or famine or nakedness or danger or sword? 36As it is written:*

"For your sake we face death all day long; we are considered as sheep to be slaughtered."

37No, in all these things we are more than conquerors through Him who loved us. 38For I am convinced that neither death nor life, neither angels nor demons, neither the present nor the future, nor any powers, 39neither height nor depth, nor anything else in all creation, will be able to separate us from the love of God that is in Christ Jesus our Lord.

How wonderful to have a Savior who does not condemn us! We have a Savior who loves us and will never leave us! We are free, truly free if we understand this truth. I am forgiven for all of my past sins, as well as my future sins. If my future sins are not forgiven I am in big trouble since all of my sins were two thousand years after Jesus died for them, they were all in the future. If I have good understanding about life in Christ then I understand that to sin brings defeat in my life. I cannot be blessed if I commit adultery. I will suffer for such a choice and so will everyone else who loves me. I cannot expect that God will bless my life if I sin. I will be blocking the blessings. Why would I want Satan to have any part of my life? Just as we need to understand who God is we need to know that Satan is out to destroy our lives. It is his aim to kill and destroy as many as he can. He is roaming around looking for possible candidates who have opened the door for him and are giving him access to their lives. I do not want to be one of them!

1 Peter 5:8 (NIV) *8Be alert and of sober mind. Your enemy the devil prowls around like a roaring lion looking for someone to devour.*

I do not believe in being so Satan minded that I am looking for him around every corner however the Bible does tell me that I need to alert and sober minded. The devil is our enemy and he does want to destroy us. We have to be aware that he does attempt to set traps that we will fall for. Keeping our eyes on Jesus and our hearts and minds focused will ensure that we do not fall for the traps that are set to destroy us.

My relationship with Christ is secure but I can open the door to evil and ruin my life. I can be the reason I am not living the abundant life that God desires for me. There are two powers at work at all times. Both want my attention but it is up to me to choose.

Romans 7: 21-25 (NIV) *21So I find this law at work: Although I want to do good, evil is right there with me. 22For in my inner being I delight in God's law; 23but I see another law at work in me, waging war against the law of my mind and making me a prisoner of the law of sin at work within me. 24What a wretched man I am! Who will rescue me from this body that is subject to death? 25Thanks be to God, who delivers me through Jesus Christ our Lord!*

There is a struggle going on for your mind. God wants you to have a renewed mind but Satan wants you as you were. The less you know about God the more access Satan has. We fail to realize that he is very capable of putting thoughts into our minds and he often does. Sin starts with a thought, a desire is born only then does it lead to death.

James 1:15 (NIV) *15After desire has conceived, it gives birth to sin; and sin, when it is full-grown, gives birth to death.*

We have to learn to stop the thought from developing. The more you know about your life in Christ and what He wants for you the better your chances are of stopping the wrong thoughts before they become a desire.

Your relationship with God is utterly important. You desperately need to have it. Life is hard and seems to be getting harder all the time. Evil is around us, everywhere you look you see it. If we want to be Daniels and be able to stand against all the evil in the world then we need to know who we are, who God is and we need a renewed mind so that we can understand and walk in victory.

We need to understand the authority we have been given. When God put Adam and Eve in the Garden of Eden he told them to subdue the earth,

Genesis 1:28 (KJV) *28And God blessed them, and God said unto them, Be fruitful, and multiply, and replenish the earth, and subdue it.*

Psalm 115:16 (NIV) *16The highest heavens belong to the Lord, but the earth he has given to mankind*

God gave the earth to mankind and we have been told to subdue it but we need to understand that Satan is the prince of the air.

Ephesians 2:1-2 (NIV) *1As for you, you were dead in your transgressions and sins, 2in which you used to live when you followed the ways of this world and of the ruler of the kingdom of the air, the spirit who is now at work in those who are disobedient.*

Jesus said that we have been given the authority over the prince of the air.

Luke 10:19 (NIV) *19I have given you authority to trample on snakes and scorpions and to overcome all the power of the enemy; nothing will harm you.*

Ephesians 6; 10-18 (NIV) *[10]Finally, be strong in the Lord and in his mighty power. [11]Put on the full armor of God, so that you can take your stand against the devil's schemes. [12]For our struggle is not against flesh and blood, but against the rulers, against the authorities, against the powers of this dark world and against the spiritual forces of evil in the heavenly realms. [13]Therefore put on the full armor of God, so that when the day of evil comes, you may be able to stand your ground, and after you have done everything, to stand. [14]Stand firm then, with the belt of truth buckled around your waist, with the breastplate of righteousness in place, [15]and with your feet fitted with the readiness that comes from the gospel of peace. [16]In addition to all this, take up the shield of faith, with which you can extinguish all the flaming arrows of the evil one. [17]Take the helmet of salvation and the sword of the Spirit, which is the word of God. [18]And pray in the Spirit on all occasions with all kinds of prayers and requests. With this in mind, be alert and always keep on praying for all the Lord's people*

God has given us everything we need to defeat Satan; we have been given authority and tools to use in the battle to stand against the devils schemes.

God gave authority to us but we fail to use what we have been given. We think the devil is some strong mighty force that we have to fight against to our dying day. Satan only has authority that you give him! If you are a child of God you have far more power than Satan does. Satan knows this is true but many Christians have yet to realize this truth. You and I have the authority to command Satan in the name of Jesus to leave and he has to go. He is not going to hang around the corner and pounce back on you as soon as you turn around. He is defeated and he knows it. The only way he is going to hang around is if you do not understand the power you have. There is great power in the name of Jesus and Satan cannot stand against it! When we use the name of Jesus and speak knowing this power is alive and active we can overcome Satan. It is in our speaking, our testimony that we have the power to overcome the devil. In Revelation 12 we find the following scripture:

They triumphed over him by the blood of the Lamb and by the word of their testimony

The power came with their testimony, we must learn to use our words and live victoriously.

We do not have to run and hide or live in fear of Satan. In Jesus name he has to flee. In Jesus name he is not quietly tip toeing out of the picture, he is fleeing! I don't have to scream and shout at him, I have authority over him and I do not have to stay up all night fighting him.

I have found this so helpful in my life. It brings me much peace to know that I can be in control of my thoughts and the power Satan has. He may put thoughts in my mind but I do not have to dwell there I can instead choose to think on the things of God. My thought life is under my control and when I understand that, I learn to recognize that when I believe a lie I can overcome it by commanding Satan in the name of Jesus to leave. My thinking and what I think on is up to me I just need to recognize when my thoughts are not lining up with the Word of God.

Understanding that Satan only has the power you give him helps you to realize that you have the choice to allow him to have power or not. It is up to each of us. Unfortunately many Christians have no idea that they have this power over him and they fight and fight against him. Satan knows he is defeated but often times we don't know it!

This reminds me of the scripture that tells us that Satan knows that God is real and he trembles.

James 2:19 (KJV) *19 Thou believest that there is one God; thou doest well: the devils also believe, and tremble*

Satan is well aware of the fact that there is one God and he fears Him. He knows he is defeated now we just need to realize it as well!

Satan also knows that his time is running out and our Lord will be returning to earth for his bride (that's us!) When Christ returns He will put an end to Satan's schemes. Christ has overcome and He has given us the power to defeat the devil as well. God is on our side and when God is on your side you can't help but be the winner, an over comer!

14

Is Your Thinking Making You Sick?

· OUT OF THE MOUTH FLOW THE
ISSUES OF THE HEART ·

Proverbs 18:21 (NIV) *²¹Death and life are in the power of the tongue: and they that love it shall eat the fruit thereof.*

There is great power in words and the words we speak bring either life or death. This includes our health. Have you ever noticed that most people, Christians included are quick to tell you everything that is wrong with their health? They will go into great detail telling you about all their aches and pains. Why do we do that? We are bringing sickness upon ourselves with our words.

This is another way that we have to change our thinking. We get so used to hearing the negative words that are spoken by others as well as by ourselves that we don't hear them anymore. If we can take every thought captive then that means we can learn to think differently about our words as well as everything else. We think sick, we speak sick and we live sick, something has to change! This is all part of renewing our minds:

Romans 12:2 (NIV) *²Do not conform to the pattern of this world, but be transformed by the renewing of your mind. Then you will be able to test and approve what God's will is—his good, pleasing and perfect will.*

God has a good, pleasing and perfect will for our lives. It is up to us to renew our way of thinking and to live the blessed life God has promised us. God does not want us sick; His people should be healthy and have long lives, that would be God's perfect will.

I realize that there will be many who are reading this that may say they can agree with the rest of this book but they cannot believe that it is Gods will for all to be healed. To them I ask "find me a scripture in the New Testament where Jesus made someone sick?" He didn't! He came and all were healed. You can see that all through the gospels. People flocked to Him and He healed them and forgave their sins.

Matthew 9:35 (NIV) *³⁵Jesus went through all the towns and villages, teaching in their synagogues, proclaiming the good news of the kingdom and healing every disease and sickness.*

Luke 6:19 (NIV) *¹⁹the people all tried to touch him, because power was coming from him and healing them all.*

Luke 9:11 (NIV) *¹¹He welcomed them and spoke to them about the kingdom of God, and healed those who needed healing*

Why is it so hard to believe that a loving father would want us to be healthy? A sick Christian cannot get up and go out and share the gospel, his testimony is of no effect. He will not be making disciples, besides who would want to serve a God that makes us sick?

Sickness comes from Satan, he is the one who is out to steal, kill and destroy. The Bible makes it perfectly clear that is what Satan does and no where will you read that description of

God. God is good and has provided healing; we fail to receive what He has provided because we don't believe.

I used to have a hard time understanding the idea of receiving your healing. Then one day as I was meditating on this and I saw it. Receiving healing is as simple as believing. If you don't believe then don't expect your healing. If you enjoy the attention you get by being sick and you like it that way, more power to you but that is not how I want to live my life and I don't believe it is how God wants me to live my life either.

Several years ago I started with lots of health problems. The problems started before my father passed away and only got worse after that. It all started when I flew to Atlanta with a viral inner ear infection that I didn't know I had. I started with terrible dizzy spells so bad that I couldn't walk without holding on to walls, chairs or something else. I couldn't go to work and I spent most of my time sitting in a recliner just trying to cope with the problems. After about three months of this my daughter suggested I see an ear, nose and throat specialist. This is when I learned about vertigo. I was blessed with a great doctor and he had me lay on a table as he rotated my head and explained that the crystals in my ears were out of place and it was causing my dizziness. He sent me home and told me to hold still for a few days. However I bent over to pick something up from the floor and the dizziness returned with a vengeance. I returned to his office two more times and finally went home and put on a neck brace and sat in my chair for three days. I did not move! I got better.

Then one day I was working and I went to one of our warehouses and when I got there I felt total confusion. I had no idea why I was there and I just stood in the driveway confused. I called my daughter who came and got me but I couldn't think straight and I started with one of the worst times I have ever had physically. At times my mind would go blank and I would just sit in confusion. I couldn't remember people's names, I forgot things I did last week, and I felt like I was losing my mind.

One day I walked out of the office into the parking lot and just stood there. I felt like I wasn't really there. My daughter saw what was happening and came out to help me. By then I couldn't talk. She called 911 while I sat in a chair without a word to say. I remember wanting to tell her not to worry but I couldn't form any words. I saw the fear in her eyes and wanted to comfort her and reassure her that I would be alright but no words came. For the first time in my life I was completely speechless, literally!

In the emergency room they started a variety of tests while I just lay there watching what was going on around me. Slowly speech started coming back but a very slow speech. As I started to feel a bit more normal they decided that I may have had a mini stroke, but they didn't believe the symptoms were all there. They didn't know what else it could be.

Time went on and I ended up in the emergency room a few more times. I started to feel the attacks coming on but couldn't think of any words to explain what I felt. Finally I was sent to see a neurologist. She asked me to describe what I felt but I couldn't. Words were just not coming and I had no idea how to communicate it. My vocabulary was somewhat limited and I just didn't know how to describe what I was feeling. My mind could not come up with the right words.

The doctor decided to see if I was having seizures. I underwent some tests but nothing showed up. She decided to put me on a low dose of medication for epilepsy to see if there were any improvements. I continued to have the attacks, so she upped the medication to a stronger dose, still they continued. Finally she upped it again and I started to feel a bit better. I was at a gathering of cousins when an attack came at the same time something else happened in the room and no one noticed that I was having the attack. The attack lasted for the duration of the other distraction in the room and then we returned to our conversation but I had no idea what we had been talking about so I had to ask. When I returned to the doctor's office she again asked if I could describe the feeling and I said "yes, it is a brain freeze." She smiled and said "you are having seizures, you have epilepsy." This began my life of medication. I was able to control my seizures which were called cluster seizures. They do not happen for about three weeks then in a period of two or three days I would have anywhere from three to ten seizures. With the medication I could control them.

My memory started to get a bit better but I did not like to be on medication and the medication made me dizzy. I believed in a God who heals but I was sick.

About a year later I was at a family gathering in a restaurant when a distant cousin who I had not met before heard that I had epilepsy, he wanted to pray for me. In the middle of the restaurant he came over to my table and sat down and began to pray for my healing. He commanded Satan and his demons to leave and not return. As he prayed I decide I was receiving my healing. I decided to believe! Praise God I have not taken one pill nor have I had any seizures since that day. I am healed. I can work, I remember, I know people's names and I walk in victory.

My healing came because I chose to believe what Gods word says is true. Not only was I healed from Epilepsy but I was also seeing an oncologist because my white blood count was not where it should have been. I had been going in about every six months for blood work and she informed me that I had cancer somewhere in my body that my body was fighting off at the time but she believed sooner or later the cancer would manifest itself. My blood count had stayed about the same for several years so she had me coming in one time a year to keep an eye on it. After I was prayed for I had an appointment with her again and when she came in to talk to me after the blood work results were done she talked about a number of things and I finally I asked her "What about my blood?" She looked at me and said "It is normal" I wanted to shout from the roof top. I was healed of two bad situations and I felt free for the first time in five years! I have since then been back to the doctor's office and she released me telling me that my body was fighting infection just as it is designed to do. Praise God I am healed!

Matthew 4:24 (NIV) *24News about him spread all over Syria, and people brought to Him all who were ill with various diseases, those suffering severe pain, the demon-possessed, those having seizures, and the paralyzed; and He healed them.*

Matthew 8:13 (NIV) *13Then Jesus said to the centurion, "Go! Let it be done just as you believed it would." And his servant was healed at that moment*

Jesus came not only to save us but to heal us; it is up to us to receive our healing.

Once again this is a place where we can use our authority. We can command Satan to take the sickness from us and thank God for the healing that He has provided. There is so much more to talk about on this and if you still doubt that healing is for today I encourage you to look for yourself, the Bible is full of healing scriptures and you will never convince me that healing isn't for today because I have been healed and I cannot tell you how wonderful it is to feel well. If you want to be sick that is your choice but I choose health and I choose to believe!

It is amazing how many people confess sickness. If you stop to consider that your words have power and what you say you will speak into existence you'll learn to be more careful of the words coming out of your mouth. There are a few people in my life that are so negative and they are constantly talking about what all is wrong with them, all their diseases and the symptoms that they are experiencing. It is so hard for me to be around them because I hear their confession; their negative words are producing exactly what they are professing.

When I catch myself saying things I shouldn't say I am disappointed in myself. If my words truly have power then I need to be speaking life into my life's problems not death. How often have we complained about things in our lives in a very negative way then we turn around and pray for the opposite to happen? Life and death are in the power of the tongue and we need to hear want we are saying and change our confession, starting with me! I'm working on this and I do catch myself and often stop but old habits die hard and it will be a battle that I will win!

Proverbs 18:21 (NIV) *21 The tongue has the power of life and death, and those who love it will eat its fruit.*

Learn to listen to what people say, and then learn to listen to what you are saying. We say the craziest things and bring disaster on ourselves. I believe that I am healthy and I confess it. I say it and I believe it. Does this mean that I never get a headache? No, but as soon as I realize that a headache is coming on I recognize that it is not from God and I command it to leave and it leaves. My words will go something like this. "No

I will not accept this, I have been healed by Jesus and I walk in health. Satan I command you in the name of Jesus to take this headache and get out of my life, you have no authority here and I take the authority that God gave me and I command you to go." Then I choose to believe that I am healed.

Sometimes I may have signs of sickness like a cold and I will do the same thing. Several weeks ago my husband had a cold and I took authority and I proclaimed that I would not get a cold. I did not get a cold. On the other hand there are times that I do not fight against the sickness and I suffer like everyone else.

There are a number of good books about healing that will help you to see into this further than I can go into here, let's face it, it would be another book! I would recommend T.L Osborne's book "Healing the Sick" or Andrew Wommack's books "Believers Authority." And "You've Already Got It" All of these books will give you a lot of understanding about this topic. You can choose to learn more or you can deny that God's healing is for today, the choice is yours.

Earlier in this book I mentioned that I felt God was asking me to do something that I have not felt comfortable with. I always know that when God asks something of me that He will give me opportunities to follow through with what He has asked of me. It is not hard for me to pray with people in church for healing but it has been hard outside the four walls of the church for me to pray for someone when I saw a need. I knew this was something I had to do. What good is a light if it is hidden, what good is an answer if it isn't shared. Of course it wasn't long until I had opportunity.

I was with my mother and a friend at breakfast one morning, in the same restaurant that I was prayed for by a cousin. Our friend mentioned that she was suffering from back pain and she had never had it before. She had a lot she wanted to do that day but her back was limiting her. I reached over and laid my hand on her and simply said "Be healed in Jesus name." We continued with breakfast. Several days later my mother was talking to her and she told her that her backache had left her the same day I prayed for her. A simple prayer offered in faith is answered by our loving father.

When you are a part of such a simple act and you see God answer a prayer it builds your faith and gives you courage to do it again. You see that God is indeed working through you. I have prayed for a number of people since that and I am making progress in what I felt the Lord wants me to do. Only when I step out and do what He asks me to do will He give me more and lead me to another step that will help me become who He wants me to be. I believe in healing and I believe we will see a lot more healing miracles in the days ahead. It is indeed a great time to be alive!

15

Do We Have Compassion?

· LOVE YOUR NEIGHBOR AS YOU LOVE YOURSELF ·

Webster describes compassion as: sympathetic consciousness of others' distress together with a desire to alleviate it. When we look at the world as a whole on the surface it would look like a very compassionate society. There are many organizations that claim to be feeding the hungry, digging wells for water for the needy, and many organizations with a long list of things that they are trying to provide for others. All of this is good when it is true but many times we find out that the claims being made are not accurate. Truly compassionate people are easily led to give because they care. Unfortunately in many cases not all the money given goes for the purpose that it is advertised for.

When we have compassion we genuinely want to alleviate the pain and suffering of others no matter who they are. We want to help ease their burden. As Christians we are taught in church to help those in need. I believe that most people who give have the right heart in giving for these purposes but we also have thousands if not millions of people who want only for themselves, they feel only their own lack although many times what they think of as lack in their lives is nothing more than greed.

Throughout the Bible we read many scriptures about the compassion of Jesus and this is where we will find what true compassion looks like. Let's take a look at some of these scriptures to see what God's version of compassion looked like in his Son.

Matthew 9:36 (NIV) *36When He saw the crowds, he had compassion on them, because they were harassed and helpless, like sheep without a shepherd.*

Matthew 14:14 (NIV) *14When Jesus landed and saw a large crowd, He had compassion on them and healed their sick.*

Jesus understood that without Him we are like lost sheep, He cared deeply for the lost and hurting. His compassion went beyond the physical and longed for eternal life for all people. He didn't want to see them suffer with sickness and disease and when He healed them He healed them in every area. He still does that for us today. He came and taught, He was hung on the cross and died, He was buried but He arose and defeated death and made eternal life a possibility for all. Just before He died on the cross He declared "It is finished". He had completed the task and now He sits at the right hand of the Father at rest, His work finished.

One of my favorite chapters in the Bible (as you can see I have many!) is Psalm 103. It talks about the compassion of God and gives us a picture of what has been done for us. As you read through this pay attention to the word "compassion".

Psalm 103

1Praise the Lord, my soul;
  all my inmost being, praise his holy name.

²Praise the Lord, my soul,
  and forget not all his benefits—
³who forgives all your sins
  and heals all your diseases,
⁴who redeems your life from the pit
  and crowns you with love and compassion,
⁵who satisfies your desires with good things
  so that your youth is renewed like the eagle's.
⁶The Lord works righteousness
  and justice for all the oppressed.
⁷He made known his ways to Moses,
  his deeds to the people of Israel:
⁸The Lord is compassionate and gracious,
  slow to anger, abounding in love.
⁹He will not always accuse,
  nor will he harbor his anger forever;
¹⁰he does not treat us as our sins deserve
  or repay us according to our iniquities.
¹¹For as high as the heavens are above the earth,
  so great is his love for those who fear him;
¹²as far as the east is from the west,
  so far has he removed our transgressions from us.
¹³As a father has compassion on his children,
  so the Lord has compassion on those who fear him;
¹⁴for he knows how we are formed,
  he remembers that we are dust.
¹⁵The life of mortals is like grass,
  they flourish like a flower of the field;
¹⁶the wind blows over it and it is gone,
  and its place remembers it no more.
¹⁷But from everlasting to everlasting

the Lord's love is with those who fear him,
  and his righteousness with their children's children—
[18]with those who keep his covenant
  and remember to obey his precepts.
[19]The Lord has established his throne in heaven,
  and his kingdom rules over all.
[20]Praise the Lord, you his angels,
  you mighty ones who do his bidding,
  who obey his word.
[21]Praise the Lord, all his heavenly hosts,
  you his servants who do his will.
[22]Praise the Lord, all his works
  everywhere in his dominion.
Praise the Lord, my soul.

We are crowned with love and compassion! God has compassion for us so much so that we are crowned with it. The Lord is compassionate and gracious and because of His great compassion for us He is slow to anger abounding in love towards us. He then shows us that as humans we have compassion for our children and He compares that to His own feelings about us. We have the Creator of the earth and everything in it showing compassion to humans that He formed out of dust that is amazing!

It is so easy for us to look down on others because we feel superior to them for one reason or another but we are all just made of dust, we are all in the same boat and without a God who has compassion on us we are nothing. God has compassion on us and we are to show and have true compassion for others.

Jesus came to the world because He had compassion for the people His Father had created. Now it is our turn to show Godly compassion to others. Love and compassion go a long way in winning the lost in our world. The question is do we have true compassion like Jesus has?

As I am writing the chapter I am looking at my own life and finding that I am not always very compassionate. It's not that I don't want to be and not that I don't believe I am called to be it is that I don't always remember how much God has done for me, I don't always remember that I am just like all other human beings and that without God I cannot have true compassion. The Holy Spirit who lives inside me helps me to live a more compassionate life. I have to learn to see others the way God sees them.

Recently I was in a large crowd of people and as I looked at the crowd the Holy Spirit stopped me and I saw what could be a sea of lost souls. As I gazed over the crowd my heart began to melt for the people. I was overcome with sadness at what I saw. These were all people, some of whom I am sure were Christians, but many were lost souls who would not spend eternity with Jesus if someone did not reach them with the good news. I prayed quietly and asked God to help me to do my part in helping to reach the lost. I had compassion for the people and that experience has changed me. I cannot be in a large group of people without remembering this experience. I want to be forever changed.

We are asked to be harvesters to bring in the harvest. Lost souls being saved is our goal. Jesus told us about this in Matthew.

Mathew 9:35-38 (NIV) *35Jesus went through all the towns and villages, teaching in their synagogues, proclaiming the good news of the kingdom and healing every disease and sickness. 36When he saw the crowds, he had compassion on them, because they were harassed and helpless, like sheep without a shepherd. 37Then he said to his disciples, "The harvest is plentiful but the workers are few. ³⁸Ask the Lord of the harvest, therefore, to send out workers into his harvest field."*

We are the workers and we have to have compassion on a lost and dying world. Many Christians have lost family members. Our love and compassion will make a difference. The harvest doesn't always come quickly just like it doesn't come quickly for the farmers, we have to plant the seed, water it and wait for the seed to take root. That is easier said than done.

We tend to go through life thinking there is nothing we can do about certain situations but we are deceived. Nothing is impossible with God and He is living inside of you.

Mark 9:23 *²³Jesus said to him, "If you can believe, all things are possible to him who believes."*

²⁴Immediately the father of the child cried out and said with tears, "Lord, I believe; help my unbelief!"

This is a story from Mark about a man who brought his sick son to Jesus and Jesus told him that if he believed that all things are possible. The man replied Lord I believe, help my unbelief. This can be confusing but think about it, how often have you prayed about something believing and knowing that God can do anything but then turned around and made a negative comment to someone that goes opposite of what you have been praying for. This is your unbelief at work. We have to wholly believe and not doubt, then nothing is impossible for us. Jesus had compassion and He overcame the situation.

If we can get a hold of this we can live the life of an over comer. We can overcome anything that comes against us but without compassion we can be so self centered that we place all the value of over coming into our own lives. When we learn that we are over comers and we have compassion we can make a big difference in the world.

If we could learn to have compassion like Jesus had when He was here the world would be a different place. He had compassion on the sick and the lost so healing them was easy. He cared in a way that very few of us care for others. Jesus loves us and we all know that, we have heard it all of our lives. We've sung the song since we were children and maybe so much so that we don't hear the words anymore. Love and compassion together are unquenchable. Have you ever been with someone you knew loved you far beyond anything you could really grasp? I think that is what it would have been like to spend time with Jesus.

I imagine looking into his eyes and seeing such love that you would be consumed by it. I picture being wrapped in it, feeling secure, and completely overcome with the thought of such love and compassion. I try to see Jesus as He might have been here on the earth, about his Father's business, healing the sick, seeing the lame walk, the blind see and the deaf hear. He was so in tune with His Father that He only did what He saw the Father doing. So the Father wanted the sick healed and the lost saved. This is stated very clearly in scripture so why would we choose to believe that God brings sickness to people? A compassionate father would never do that.

John 5:19 (NIV) *¹⁹Jesus gave them this answer: "Very truly I tell you, the Son can do nothing by Himself; He can do only what He sees his Father doing, because whatever the Father does the Son also does.*

God is full of compassion for His children and we are all His children. There is no one that was not formed by God therefore we are all His children. The problem is that not all of us recognize Him as our Creator, our Father; we do not accept what He has done for us. We do not all see the love of God or the compassion He has. Many are blind choosing not to believe, others haven't heard the good news of Jesus.

We as believers are the hands and the feet of Jesus. We are to spread the good news; we are to bring in the harvest. We need to start seeing others the way Jesus does; we need to be compassionate and full of love, overcoming things that others see as obstacles. Instead of being quick to condemn we need to love. It is love that never fails, not condemnation.

· JESUS WAS FULL OF COMPASSION ·

Psalm 86:15 (NIV) *15But you, Lord, are a compassionate and gracious God, slow to anger, abounding in love and faithfulness*

Psalm 116:5 (NIV) *5The Lord is gracious and righteous; our God is full of compassion*

If we want to reach people then we need to change how we represent God. Screaming hell, fire and brimstone is not the way Jesus reached out to the lost instead He had compassion on them.

People who have near death experiences talk about the feeling of total acceptance they felt in the presence of Jesus. No condemnation, no guilt just surrounded by love and compassion.

Sometimes I see something on television that brings out this feeling in me that I would call compassion. I am sure this happens to most of us. I will see a story about starving children or communities without clean drinking water, sick dying children in countries with no medical care and I almost cannot watch them because I feel so small and helpless. The problems look so big and we think the little money we can give will never make a difference. What we have to remember is that the little we give is not little when God gets hold of it. It reminds me of the story of the loaves and fish.

Mark 6:38-44 (NIV) *38"How many loaves do you have?" he asked. "Go and see."*

When they found out, they said, "Five—and two fish."

[39]Then Jesus directed them to have all the people sit down in groups on the green grass. [40]So they sat down in groups of hundreds and fifties. [41]Taking the five loaves and the two fish and looking up to heaven, He gave thanks and broke the loaves. Then He gave them to His disciples to distribute to the people. He also divided the two fish among them all. [42]They all ate and were satisfied, [43]and the disciples picked up twelve basketfuls of broken pieces of bread and fish. [44]The number of the men who had eaten was five thousand.

Everything is different when Jesus is in the picture! Never underestimate the power of God. Having compassion compels us to give when we see a need. The amount isn't the point; the motive behind the gift is what matters.

True compassion doesn't forget the pain others are going through, it moves us to give where it is needed. True compassion will make you talk to the lost about Jesus because we don't want to see them lost forever. True compassion moves us to pray with the sick and teach them about a loving God who doesn't want them to be sick. True compassion sees that we can overcome all of these things; we just need the teaching so that we can understand.

When we really see what is happening to those around us who are not saved and we know what their future is we should be moved by such love that we risk being rejected by them in hopes that we can help them to see the truth, the truth that will set them free.

As I think about praying for the sick I see myself moving out and not being so fearful of being rejected. There are very few people who are seriously sick that will not want you to pray for them. Seriously ill people don't want to be sick they want to enjoy life. No one wants to spend time in a cancer ward; no one wants to be hospitalized for any reason. Knowing this should fill us with the courage we need to step out and pray for them.

Reading through the book of Ephesians you can see that these things have already been provided. Paul the author of Ephesians prays for us to understand what we have been given.

Ephesians 1:18-20 (NIV) *18I pray that the eyes of your heart may be enlightened in order that you may know the hope to which he has called you, the riches of his glorious inheritance in his holy people, 19and his incomparably great power for us who believe. That power is the same as the mighty strength 20he exerted when he raised Christ from the dead and seated him at his right hand in the heavenly realms,*

We have within us the same power that raised Jesus from the dead! That is a lot of power, but we aren't using it. Why? Paul is praying for us to have understanding. Paul understood some things that we make hard to believe. Why can we not just take the words of Jesus for what they are? Why do we have to try to read into things and make excuses for our lack of power? If we are living without this power it is because of a lack of understanding. Without power you will never overcome. Oh God open our eyes to see the truth for what it is!

Because of Paul's upbringing he spent a lot of time memorizing scripture; it was part of his education as a young boy. After his encounter with Jesus he spent several years alone with God, during that time he gained understanding and he discovered the love and compassion of God. It is what made him so brave to go out and spread the news he understood. He knew things because he experienced things with God. He tries to teach us what he understood but we make it hard. Paul was afraid of no one and he endured a lot of persecution for what he taught. He taught what he believed, he taught what he knew was true.

The Word of God is sometimes offensive to others. People will be offended; we see it all the time in today's world. That is Satan at work deceiving the people whose hearts are hard. Only love and compassion will melt those cold hearts. Often we look at people of the world and see their success and it appears that they are the ones that have overcome, they have been successful. But success is more than having money. Often times these people have been married several times, they and their children are often into drugs and alcohol, they have many problems that we do not know about, that is not the life of an over comer. On the surface it can all look so good, but underneath it all there is no true success.

God blesses us so that we can be a blessing. God wants us to be over comers and He wants us to have compassion. If we have compassion we can be a blessing and we will overcome the world! If we had the compassion Jesus had we would be out front being the forerunner bringing the good news to the lost and seeing souls saved.

There is a great harvest out there ready to be harvested but without the harvesters there is no harvest. For all of us who have lost family members, we need to pray for the harvesters and we have to be willing to be the harvesters when we have the opportunity to reach the lost. Pray for your children who are grown that they would be reminded of the things they learned in Sunday school, pray for the Holy Spirit to bring things to remembrance that they were taught at some point in life that will become real to them and pray for the harvester who has compassion and will reach out to your loved ones. We need to pray that their eyes will be opened and their hearts softened. It is often hard to reach your own adult children. We have compassion for them and we yearn for their salvation but often it will take someone else to bring them home. Remember you could be the harvester for someone else's loved one, don't miss the opportunity to be used by God.

I would guess that for most Christians it is easier to offer to pray for the sick than to try to reach out to the lost. The sick know they need help but the lost sometimes choose to be lost. Is it not our goal to be Christ like? Are we even trying to be like Christ or have we just decided that it is not possible so why try so hard?

Philippians 2:1-3 (NIV) *Therefore if you have any encouragement from being united with Christ, if any comfort from his love, if any common sharing in the Spirit, if any tenderness and compassion, ²then make my joy complete by being like-minded, having the same love, being one in spirit and of one mind. ³Do nothing out of selfish ambition or vain conceit. Rather, in humility value others above yourselves*

The description of Christ in these scriptures paints a picture of what our lives should look like, is there any resemblance? We are to be like-minded, like Christ in our thinking. For most of us there is a long road ahead of changing our thinking to be like minded.

Let us each make a commitment that we will make it our life's goal to be like-minded just as we are told to be. To reach those goals we need to grow up, change our thinking and take responsibility for the things we can change. We need to know what the word of God says then put to practice what we learn, and teach others to also be Christ like. Our actions speak volumes and so do the words we say, the things we confess tells others what we believe or don't believe. We need to guard our words and learn to think before we talk.

We need to show the world what compassion looks like,

what love looks like, who Jesus is by how we live our lives. They are watching, they are seeing who we are and they are judging Christianity when they see our behavior or hear our words. If you have compassion the world will see it.

Have you ever wondered how non-Christians would describe Christians? Would they say we are judgmental and hypocritical? Many would call us narrow minded and old fashioned. We need to change what they are seeing. Our testimony is being voided by our behavior and attitude. Our words give us away and people judge us by what we say and how we act and react.

As followers of Christ we need to be aware of how we think and talk. We need to be compassionate and loving when we see the lost and the hurting around us. We need to care!

When we truly learn to love each other we will become compassionate people. The world will know us by our behavior.

When our son left his wife and children we were devastated. We didn't see it coming and were blind sighted by this event. Eventually he moved to another city and he is now with another woman. I cannot tell you how hard it was for me to meet this lady. I blamed her for what had happened and had no desire to meet her. Our son insisted that she really wanted to be a part of our family and he insisted that we meet her. After a number of years I finally gave in and we took the entire family, her included to see a Broadway play. It was our first meeting. It was a good way to meet for the first time since we didn't really have time to sit down and talk one on one. Sometime later he brought her to our home for Easter. Then this last year she came for Christmas. What I have discovered in the process is that she is a nice person. I don't agree with her lifestyle but it is not up to me to preach at her and try to set her straight. I developed compassion for her because I began to realize that she most likely had not been taught anything different. Today I can say I like her, and I pray for her because I realize that if she doesn't meet Jesus before she dies she will not be in heaven and I don't want that to happen. As a family we have an opportunity to show her Jesus by how we act, talk and react to her. We may be the only Christians she will meet and the impact we can have on her could have an eternal effect. I developed compassion for her when I started to pray for her.

John 15:12-15 (NIV) *12My command is this: Love each other as I have loved you. 13Greater love has no one than this: to lay down one's life for one's friends. 14You are my friends if you do what I command.*

God didn't tell us this would always be easy but not much in life is easy, the command says "Love each other as I have loved you" I am sure I am not always loveable either! Yet He loves me.

16

Believing is a Choice

I cannot make you believe anything I say. You can choose to believe anything you want. God does not force us to do anything and that includes the choice as to whether or not we choose to believe in Him or to believe what His word says. Even Thomas, a disciple of Jesus had a hard time believing and went as far as to say that until he saw Jesus he wouldn't believe;

John 20:24-25 (NIV) *²⁴Now Thomas (also known as Didymus), one of the Twelve, was not with the disciples when Jesus came. ²⁵So the other disciples told him, "We have seen the Lord!"*

But he said to them, "Unless I see the nail marks in his hands and put my finger where the nails were, and put my hand into his side, I will not believe."

Believing is a choice and Thomas chose not to believe until he saw. I love the words of Jesus when he finally appeared to Thomas.

Vs. 29 *²⁹Then Jesus told him, "Because you have seen me, you have believed; blessed are those who have not seen and yet have believed."*

When I choose to believe without having to see Jesus in the flesh I am blessed. When I choose to believe what the

Word of God says without actually hearing God's audible voice declaring it to me I am blessed. I love hearing from God and having God encounters but I may not have those things happening daily, weekly or even once a year. I choose to simply believe because I read it in the Word and I choose to believe what it says. Everyone wants to be blessed but not all choose to believe. We all know people who have heard the Word taught but they refuse to believe because they cannot see.

What we have to learn is to believe and see with our spiritual eyes. With my natural eyes I may not be able to see God but I can see what He has created and I can without much effort realize that the sunsets, the oceans, the mountains and all of nature was not made by man. There has to be a greater power. Man can create some things but all of these things are things that no man can reproduce or create.

Recently a famous astronaut passed away who had walked on the moon. I try to imagine what it might be like to be in space and look back at the earth. How would it feel to be so far from home and see the earth? Seeing the earth from the moon would be an incredible experience and seeing the vastness of space knowing that the tiny part you see is a drop in the bucket of the entire universe God created, how small would it make you feel? How could you be in space and have such an awesome experience and not believe in a higher power? Our world is so magnificent that no man could ever have designed it.

We hear people talking about humans destroying the earth and predicting what will happen with global warming, and pollution. I sometimes wonder what God thinks when He hears these things. God created an earth that will withstand anything humans can do to it. Before God created man He already knew what they would do to the earth, He knew the earth would be populated with more than seven billion people and He made an earth that can endure what He planned. Only God will decide if and when to destroy it.

God made the universe and set it up in a system that works. The moon does not collide with the earth because God created the orbit of the planets. It works to perfection. God's handiwork is all around us and everyone can plainly see it yet some refuse to believe.

· GOD IS A SPIRIT ·

John 4:24 (NIV) *24God is spirit, and his worshipers must worship in the Spirit and in truth."*

In Genesis we read that the spirit of God hovered over the deep, spirit existed before the physical. The body you can see is the housing for your spirit while you are here on earth. The spirit does not die but the body does. When I got saved I became new in my spirit. If I look at my body after I got saved it was still the same. My personality didn't change and my character didn't change, it was in my spirit that I became a new creation my mind becomes new as I learn from God and I take time to renew my thinking and my speech. We need to learn to see ourselves as God sees us and that is in the spirit.

2 Corinthians 5:17 (NIV) *17Therefore, if anyone is in Christ, the new creation has come: The old has gone, the new is here!*

When you renew your mind to Gods way of thinking then you change from the inside out. It is your thought life, how you see things and your understanding of God that becomes renewed. This is the beginning of dynamic living!

When I can see myself as God sees me I begin to understand several truths about myself from scripture. When we take time to study scripture we discover who we truly are. I highly recommend Andrew Wommack's book Spirit, Soul and Body for a clear picture of this truth.

I choose to believe in God, I choose to believe what His Word says is true. When the Bible teaches that we have been healed I choose to believe it. When it says that my sins have been forgiven, I choose to believe it. When it says that Jesus was born of a virgin, came to earth as a man, died and rose again, I choose to believe it. In my spirit I know this is true although I did not live to see any of it.

In our thinking we cannot imagine that the people who walked with Jesus in the physical didn't believe. I try to imagine what it might have been like to walk and live with Jesus in person every day. Often we tend to think that if we had been here when Jesus walked the earth we would surely have believed. How hard would it have been to believe that a person you can see and walk and talk to in person is the Son of God? Would we be just like they were and think he is a great prophet? My guess is that we would have been no different than they were. If He came today and walked in the physical most of us would look at Him just as they did in Bible times. It all takes faith to believe and the Holy Spirit draws us to Himself.

John 6:44 (NIV) *44 "No one can come to me unless the Father who sent me draws them"*

You cannot possibly please God without having faith and believing what the Word tells us to be true.

Hebrews 11:6 (NIV) *6 And without faith it is impossible to please God, because anyone who comes to him must believe that he exists and that he rewards those who earnestly seek him.*

Romans 10:9 (NIV) *9 If you declare with your mouth, "Jesus is Lord," and believe in your heart that God raised him from the dead, you will be saved. 10 For it is with your heart that you believe and are justified, and it is with your mouth that you profess your faith and are saved. ¹¹As Scripture says, "Anyone who believes in Him will never be put to shame." ¹²For there is no difference between Jew and Gentile—the same Lord is Lord of all and richly blesses all who call on Him, ¹³for, "Everyone who calls on the name of the Lord will be saved."*

The idea of believing without seeing is a foreign thought to most people today. You hear it all the time, "I'll believe it when I see it." Everyone wants physical proof of things before they believe. To believe in God and what He has done for us, to believe that we are who God says that we are, takes faith.

Jesus will return to earth and set up his kingdom. He will rule and reign on this earth regardless of what anyone believes. The day will come when everyone will believe because they see Him arriving in the clouds just as the Bible tells us He will, but then it will be too late. God asks us to believe now, before He sends His Son back to earth to fulfill end time prophecy.

In the meantime the Kingdom of God dwells within us. We are the reality of His kingdom. It is up to us to choose to be a part of this Kingdom from within. The Spirit of God lives inside of me and He wants to live inside of you as well. I depend on the Spirit of God to lead me, to guide me and to show me which way to go. That doesn't mean that I do it right all the time, the physical natural part of me wants to take over at every opportunity. I blow it but it doesn't make me any less a child of God. I have been accepted by God, I am highly favored by God, I am the righteousness of God through Christ Jesus, the Bible tells me all of this and I choose to believe it, you can too.

It is as simple as a choice to believe. To believe you have to know what the Bible teaches about who you are. You are not going to know without spending time with God, reading His letter to you. You can learn about God from good Biblical teachers and books. Keep in mind that there are many books to choose from and if you want to know the truth you need to always check the words of man with the words of God. The more time you spend in the Word of God the more truth you will have. In your spirit you will begin to discern truth from lies.

A new way of thinking comes with hearing the Word of God, reading the Word of God and meditating on the Word of God. Your natural mind may fight against it because it is new to you but choose to believe and you will have a new life, an abundant life, a blessed life, a dynamic life!

To accept Jesus as Lord of your life and to start living this new blessed life, talk to God. If you want you can kneel, you can stand or sit, God isn't choosy about this. What God wants is your heart. Tell him that you are choosing to believe His word, invite Him into your heart and accept that the Spirit of God is living inside of you.

If you need help with this I am including a short prayer to help you. Keep in mind that repeating words that you do not believe won't change anything, the change comes with believing.

"Jesus, I come to you because I know that I am a sinner. Today I want to lay down my old life and begin a new life with you. Forgive me for the way I have been living in sin. I choose to believe that you are the son of God, that you came to earth and lived as a man that you died and rose again so that I might have eternal life. Come into my heart and be Lord of my Life. Amen"

Nothing in your life will change till you make Jesus Lord of your life and you take action to renew your mind. If you prayed the above prayer you are now saved but many people are saved without living a victorious life. You can only renew your mind to a new way of thinking by absorbing the Word of

God in your Bible. If you don't know where to start, start in Matthew and read the first four books of the New Testament. These books tell the story of Jesus' time here on earth from four different people who knew Him and walked with Him. These four gospels tell of the author's experiences with Jesus while He was here. You will learn about the love He has for you and you will see that He desires for you to have a wonderful life in the here and now. Many Christians are waiting for heaven to enjoy the good life but Jesus said the Kingdom is now. After you have read these four books you can continue by reading the rest of the New Testament. You will get into the meat of the good news and renewing your mind will be a work in progress.

You can also find several very good Bible teachers on television. Look for Christian channels and remember even there not everything is always right. We are all human and some teachers have different beliefs and interpret scripture differently. Always go back to the Bible and see for yourself if what they are teaching is in line with the Bible. If it does not line up find a different teacher. Remember also that if there is a check in your spirit about something you are hearing go elsewhere. TV preachers have often gotten a bad rap because of the few that are on begging for money promising that God will answer your prayers if you give. That is not how God works, find a different channel and watch something that feeds you truth.

Go to your local gospel book store and ask for good reading materials for new Christians. Don't look for the hard to understand teaching that a Christian who has been serving the Lord for many years may understand but you may not be ready for. You are a new Christian and as such you start out with the basic truths and grow into maturity.

In Hebrews we can read about milk for new Christians and

adult food for seasoned believers. Start at the beginning and grow into adult food, more in depth teaching. Keep growing in God, don't stop at milk!

Today is a good time to start living as God intended. Welcome to the Kingdom! The choice is yours!

Joshua 24:15 (NIV) *15But if serving the Lord seems undesirable to you, then choose for yourselves this day whom you will serve, whether the gods your ancestors served beyond the Euphrates, or the gods of the Amorites, in whose land you are living. But as for me and my household, we will serve the Lord!"*

Other books
BY JO ANN SCHROCK-HERSHBERGER

Challenges, Choices & Changes
Change Begins with Me

If you enjoyed this book, be sure to visit principles4freedom.com for more great products, inspirational blog posts, and other great content.

For additional copies of this or other books by this author, visit bookcentra.com

For more info on the values and principles of La Red visit www.lared.org

Read the story of Jo Ann's father, John Schrock, who was raised in an Amish home. As a child, John had a desire to change the world. His love for people never changed and his life and words have reached across the globe and are still making a difference in the lives of thousands of people in many nations. His story will inspire you to make a difference; God will use a willing vessel. John passed away in November of 2011 but his work continues to change lives.

Jo Ann Schrock-Hershberger

CHANGE
begins with
ME

Living by the Principles

This book will take you through the forty principles found in Proverbs that John Schrock, Jo Ann's father, developed into a worldwide program called La Red. Stories of Jo Ann's own life, including overcoming obstacles, and living at peace though things around her were not always peaceful, are used throughout the book. Learn to apply these simple, yet profound truths to your own life and change the world one person at a time, starting with yourself.